Admiral Matelieff's Singapore and Johor (1606-1616)

Admiral Matelieff's Singapore and Johor (1606-1616)

Edited, annotated and introduced by
Peter Borschberg

NUS PRESS
SINGAPORE

Published by:

NUS Press
National University of Singapore
AS3-01-02, 3 Arts Link
Singapore 117569
Fax: (65) 6774-0652
E-mail: nusbooks@nus.edu.sg
Website: http://nuspress.nus.edu.sg

ISBN 978-981-4722-18-6 (paper)
eISBN 978-981-09-5938-8

First edition 2016
Reprint 2017

National Library Board, Singapore Cataloguing in Publication Data

Names: Matelief, Cornelis, de jonge, 1570-1632. | Borschberg, Peter, editor.
Title: Admiral Matelieff's Singapore and Johor (1606-1616) / edited, annotated and introduced by Peter Borschberg.
Description: Singapore: NUS Press, [2016] | Includes bibliographical references and index. | Original texts translated from Dutch.
Identifiers: OCN 953678709 | ISBN 978-981-47-2218-6 (paperback)
Subjects: LCSH: Matelief, Cornelis, de jonge, 1570-1632--Travel. | Singapore--History--17th century. | Johor (Malaysia)--History--17th century.
Classification: DDC 959.503--dc23

Cover image: Undated view of Tondano from the diary of Governor Padt-Brugge (The Hague, National Archives of the Netherlands, 4.VEL 1305).

Printed by: Mainland Press Pte Ltd

Contents

List of Abbreviations

BOC	Pieter van Dam, *Beschryvinge van de Oostindische Compagnie*, ed. by F.W. Stapel, 8 vols. (The Hague: Martinus Nijhoff, 19931-43).
BV	Isaac Commelin, *Begin ende Voortgang Vande Vereenigde Neerlandsche Geoctroyeerde Oost-Indische Compagnie*, 4 vols., facsimile reproduction of the original printed in Amsterdam in 1646 in 2 vols. (Amsterdam: Facsimile Uitgaven Nederland, 1969).
CMJ	Peter Borschberg, ed., and R. Roy trans., *Journal, Memorials and Letters of Cornelis Matelieff de Jonge: Security, Diplomacy and Commerce in 17th Century Southeast Asia* (Singapore: NUS Press, 2015).
CSDI	Garcia da Orta, *Colloquies on the Simple and Drugs of India*, trans. Clements Markham, reprint of the original edition of 1913 (Delhi: Sri Satguru Publications, 1987).
EFS	Anthony Farrington and Dhiravat na Pombejra, ed., *The English Factory in Siam, 1612-1685*, 2 vols. (London: The British Library, 2007).
GLA	Mons. Sebastião Rodolfo Dalgado, *Glosário Luso-Asiático*, 2 vols. (Coimbra: Imprensa da Universidade, 1919-21).
GPFT	Peter Borschberg, Hugo Grotius, *the Portuguese and Free Trade in the East Indies* (Singapore and Leiden: NUS Press and KITLV Press, 2011).
GVOC	VOC Glossarium. *Verklaringen van Termen, verzameld uit de Rijksgeschiedkundige Publicatiën*

	die betrekking hebben op de Verenigde Oost-Indische Compagnie (The Hague: Instituut voor Nederlandse Geschiedenis, 2000).
HJ	Henry Yule and A.C. Burnell, *Hobson-Jobson: A Glossary of Colloquial Anglo-Indian Words and Phrases*, reprint (Sittingbourne: Linguasia, 1994).
JCSJ	Peter Borschberg, ed., *Jacques de Coutre's Singapore and Johor (c.1594-1625)* (Singapore: NUS Press, 2015).
JDC	Peter Borschberg, ed., *The Memoirs and Memorials of Jacques de Coutre. Security, Trade and Society in 16th and 17th Century Southeast Asia* (Singapore: NUS Press, 2014).
JMBRAS	*Journal of the Malaysian Branch of the Royal Asiatic Society.*
JO	J.K.J. de Jonge, *Opkomst van het Nederlandsch gezag in Oost-Indië. Verzameling van onuitgegeven stukken uit het oud-coloniaal archief*, 16 vols. (The Hague: Martinus Nijhoff, 1866-1909).
JSEAS	*Journal of Southeast Asian Studies.*
MGED	Manuel Godhinho de Erédia, *Description of Malaca, Meridional India and Cathay. Translated from the Portuguese with Notes*, trans. and ed. J.V.G. Mills (Kuala Lumpur: MBRAS, 1997).
PSM	Paulo Jorge de Sousa Pinto, *The Portuguese and the Straits of Melaka, 1575-1619. Power, Trade and Diplomacy* (Singapore: NUS Press, 2012).
RWME	Pieter Gerritsz. Rouffaer, "Was Malaka Emporium vóór 1400 A.D. genaamd Malajoer? En waar lag Woerawari, Ma-Hasin, Langka, Batoesawar?," *Bijdragen en Mededelingen van*

	het Koninklijk Instituut voor Taal-, Land- und Volkenkunde, 77 (1921): 1-174 and 359-604.
SMS	Peter Borschberg, *The Singapore and Melaka Straits. Violence, Security and Diplomacy in the 17th Century* (Singapore and Leiden: NUS Press and KITLV Press, 2010).
UUM	Yock Fang Liaw, ed., *Undang-undang Melaka. A Critical Edition* (The Hague: De Nederlandsche Boek- en Steendrukkerij V/H H.L. Smits, 1976).
VOC	Vereenigde Oost-Indische Compagnie; United Netherlands East India Company; the Dutch East India Company.

List of Illustrations

Overleaf: Hand-drawn map of Southeast Asia and the South China Sea from Malaya to southern Japan dating from the 17th century by an unknown artist. The Hague: National Archives of the Netherlands, 4.VEL 290.

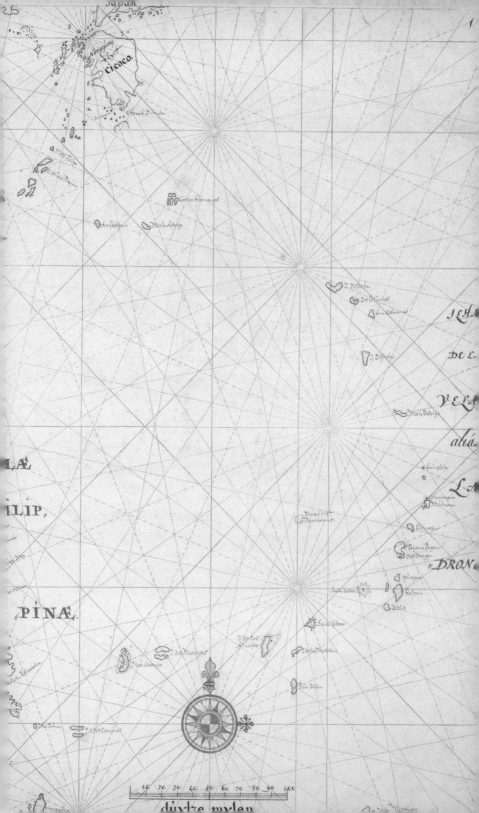

Acknowledgements

Some of the research contained in this book was facilitated by a grant awarded by Singapore's Ministry of Education and the Faculty of Arts and Social Sciences of the National University of Singapore (R110-000-052-112), research and translation funds from the National Archives of Singapore (National Heritage Board), as well as a generous donation by the Lee Foundation, Singapore. A special thanks is extended to the international research and graduate training project "Baltic Borderlands" (IRTG 1540) based at the University of Greifswald and funded by the German Research Foundation (Deutsche Forschungsgemeinschaft, DFG).

Several depository institutions played an important role in facilitating access to manuscript materials and rare prints. This includes the National Archives of the Netherlands in The Hague, Leiden University Library, the Municipal Archives (*Gemeentearchief*) of Rotterdam, the Royal Library (KB) in The Hague, as well as the Toyo Bunko (Oriental Library) in Tokyo.

The initial translation of the original texts was done by a professional Dutch translator who does not wish to be named. This was then corrected and carefully reworked, simplifying and breaking up the long early-modern sentences to make the texts more accessible to a contemporary reader. In completing these, I have relied on a number of senior and junior colleagues who have given input according to their fields of expertise.

I have benefitted from discussing the Matelieff materials with several colleagues in Asia, Australia and Europe over many years. In this context I wish to thank Adam Clulow (Monash), Alexander Drost (Greifswald), Mohd. Effendy bin Abdul Hamid (Hawaii and NUS), Maik Fiedler (Greifswald), Khir Johari (Singapore), Koh Keng We (Nanyang Technological University, NTU, and formerly at Seoul National University), Kwa Chong Guan (S. Rajaratnam School, NTU), Manuel Lobato (Portuguese Tropical Research Institute, IICT, Lisbon), Anthony Milner (Institute of Strategic and International Studies, Kuala Lumpur, and Australian National University), Henk Nellen (Constantijn-Huygens-Instituut, The Hague, and Erasmus University Rotterdam), Nordin Hussin (Universiti Kembangsaan Malaysia), Hielke van Nieuwenhuize (Greifswald), Michael North (Greifswald), Roderich Ptak (LMU, Munich), Merle Ricklefs (formerly NUS), Jörn Sander (Greifswald), Sarafian Salleh (Singapore), Lasse Seebeck (Greifswald) and António Vasconcelos de Saldanha (Macao). A special thanks to Dale Edmonds (Singapore) for the layout and Jimmy Yap (Singapore) for copyediting and preparing the text for publication.

Copyediting and layout was made possible through a generous donation from Khir Johari, Singapore, as well as another individual who wishes to remain anonymous.

Peter Borschberg
Visiting Professor
Asia-Europe Institute
University of Malaya

Preface

This publication offers a selection of reworked passages excerpted from the *Journal, Memorials and Letters of Cornelis Matelieff de Jonge* (2015) to which some new supporting documents have been added. This book is aimed at students, teachers and researchers of Southeast Asia interested in the history of Singapore, Johor and the Straits region before 1800. The introduction has been adapted from a public paper held on the occasion of the original book's soft-launch at the Siam Society in Bangkok, Thailand, on 7 August, 2014, as well as a public paper presented at the Toyo Bunko (Oriental Library) in Tokyo, Japan, on 20 September, 2014.

This book focuses on the Singapore-Johor River nexus during the first two decades of the 17th century. It should be read as an introduction or companion volume to the afore-mentioned edition of Cornelis Matelieff de Jonge's works. The glossary and list of place names have been edited and reworked to fit the format and the objectives of this publication. These glossaries offer information about functionaries, commodities and places mentioned in the texts. This information may not be readily available in English or may be difficult to source via reference works or the internet.

Did Singapore and the towns along the Johor River look something like this? Undated view of Tondano from the diary of Governor Padt-Brugge. The Hague, National Archives of the Netherlands, 4.VEL 1305.

Allegory of the Dutch East India Company as an instrument of War and Seaborne Commerce taken from a map of Batavia, dated 1665. The Hague: National Archives of the Netherlands, 4.VELH 619-32.

Introduction

Few European sources touch on the history of the Singapore-Johor nexus in the period before 1800. The vast majority of references are casual and insubstantial, frequently limited to a few words or a few lines here and there. Materials that have something more substantial to say are fewer still. Taken together, the travelogue, memorials and letters of Dutch Admiral Cornelis Matelieff de Jonge (c.1570-1632) can be considered one of the most substantial and important testimonies to survive.

More significantly perhaps, these writings help answer one of the most puzzling questions concerning the history of early modern Singapore, namely, why was Singapore's strategic location along key maritime arteries supposedly only seen in the early 19th century? Matelieff's writings reveal that the potential of Singapore's location was clearly recognized and acknowledged much earlier. More to the point: locations around the Johor River estuary were at one stage seriously considered as a potential site for the Dutch East India Company's (VOC)[1] main Asian base. As we know, the Dutch chose Jeyakerta situated on the northwestern coast of Java and renamed it Batavia in 1619. This choice, however, was the outcome of trial and error, and arguably some unique political opportunities that unfolded during the second decade of the 17th century. Though Matelieff's

---

1   See also the glossary (VOC).

1

HVGO GROTIVS

Left: Portrait of Hugo Grotius from around the year 1613. Copy by Jan van Ravensteijn based on the original in the Collection Rothschild in Paris. Leiden University Library, Icones 66.

own choice eventually fell on the town of Jeyakerta[2] almost a decade before the VOC took possession of this town by force, his shortlist of possible locations included one around the Singapore-Johor nexus. One might therefore claim that Singapore had a near miss, and one cannot help but wonder how different the history of the region might have been had the Dutch decided to establish their Asian base in the region of the Singapore Straits rather than in northwestern Java.

This book explores the history of the Singapore-Johor nexus through the writings of Cornelis Matelieff. His voyage to Southeast and East Asia took place between May 1605 and September 1608 and was conducted under the flag of the VOC. It brought the admiral into direct contact with the region around Singapore, especially Johor's capital Batu Sawar. As Matelieff is not a name familiar to many researchers of Southeast Asia, a bit of background on the man and his voyage is necessary. The introductory and biographical remarks prepare the ground for exploring his writings as important sources for the history of Singapore, Johor and the adjacent straits at the dawn of the 17th century.

Admiral and merchant

Who was Admiral Matelieff, and why is he an interesting figure historically? Cornelis Matelieff de Jonge—sometimes Cornelis Cornelisz. Matelieff or Cornelis Matelieff Junior—was born around 1570 into a respectable, but by no means wealthy, family in Rotterdam.[3] It seems that his father

2   See also the glossary (*Jeyakerta*).
3   For Matelieff's biography, see the older article by J.G. Frederiks, "Cornelis Cornelisz Matelieff de Jonge en zijn geslagt," *Rotter-*

had married into money. Cornelis Junior enjoyed a decent education and formally qualified as a draftsman.[4] Following his involvement with several smaller ventures (one which was merged into the VOC as the Rotterdam chamber),[5] Matelieff served on the Rotterdam board and, briefly, on the central board of directors, the Gentlemen Seventeen, both before and after his voyage to Asia.

Matelieff assumed the supreme command as admiral of the second fleet to be equipped and dispatched to the East Indies by the newly-formed VOC. The voyage was to last from May 1605 to early September 1608. Equipped at the very substantial cost of 2.1 million guilders,[6] the fleet received sets of both commercial and military instructions that foresaw a full-scale attack on Portuguese Melaka with the active support and assistance of the VOC's Johorese allies.[7] The joint military campaign of 1606 did not succeed

---

damsche Historie-bladen, J.H. Scheffer and Fr. D.O. Obreen, ed., 3 afd., 1.1 (1871): 204-357; and more recent research by Leo Akvelt, ed., *Machtsstrijd om Malakka. De reis van VOC-admiraal Cornelis Cornelisz. Matelief naar Oost-Azië, 1605-1608* (Zutphen: Walburg Pers, 2013).

4   Concerning his qualification as a draftsman, see M.J. Bok, "European Artists in the Service of the Dutch East India Company," in *Mediating Netherlandish Art and Material Culture in Asia*, ed. T. da Costa Kaufmann and M. North (Amsterdam: Amsterdam University Press, 2014), 196. A map of Melaka now preserved in the Bibliothèque nationale de France has been ascribed to him as one of his works. See CMJ, 173.

5   See also the glossary (*voorcompagnie*).

6   J.P. de Korte, *The Annual Accounting in the VOC, the English Companion to De Korte, De jaarlijkse financiële verantwoording in de VOC*, trans. L.F. van Lookeren Campagne-de Korte (Amsterdam: NEHA, 2000).

7   Arnold van Wickeren has in fact contended that Matelieff's objectives that had been spelt out by the Heren XVII were primarily military and not commercial in nature. See A. van Wickeren, *Geschiedenis van Portugal en van de Portugezen*

Overleaf: Bird's-eye view of Fort Orange on the island of Ternate founded by Admiral Matelieff in 1607. This depiction probably dates from the latter half of the 17th century. The Hague: National Archives of the Netherlands, 4.VEL 1313.

in wresting Melaka from Portuguese control though. A confluence of factors played a role here: insufficient gunpowder and ammunition; the reluctance of the Company's Malay allies to engage the Portuguese in hand-to-hand combat; and the arrival from Goa of, what was at the time, the largest Portuguese armada to sail the waters of the East Indies.

Even though the Dutch failed to take Melaka, Matelieff engaged the Portuguese viceroy at sea and chased the remains of his armada up to Pulau Butom. They stopped the pursuit because they were unable to lure the Portuguese into open waters from their protected anchorage at Ko A Dang in present-day Thailand.[8] After retreating to Pulau Pinang (Penang), Matelieff split up his fleet according to the instructions he had received from the VOC directors: three ships headed via Aceh[9] to India to procure textiles, while the remaining vessels headed for the Malukus, which are part of the group of islands in the eastern Indonesian Archipelago known as the Spice Islands. On the island of Ternate, Matelieff signed a treaty with its freshly-installed young ruler and founded a Dutch fort at Malayo (sometimes Malayur).

From Ternate he proceeded, as instructed, to China where he hoped to open up trade for the Dutch. After a futile attempt to strike up commerce along the Fujian coast near

---

overzee, part XVI (Heerhugowaart: no publisher, 2007), 53.

8   See also the list of place names (*Pulau Butom*).

9   Aceh was a river, port and polity in northern Sumatra. It was especially important in the context of the pepper trade. Other commodities commonly sold in Aceh included nutmeg, mace and cloves, cotton pieces, as well as opium. See CMJ, 526; JDC, 349-50.

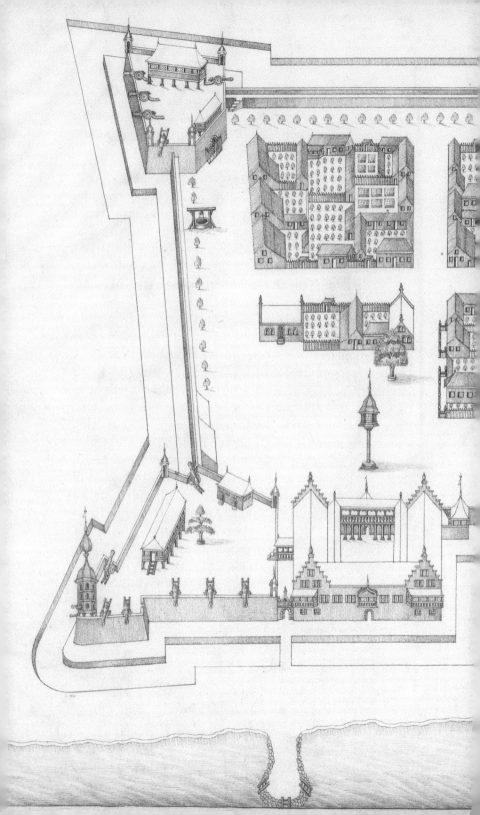

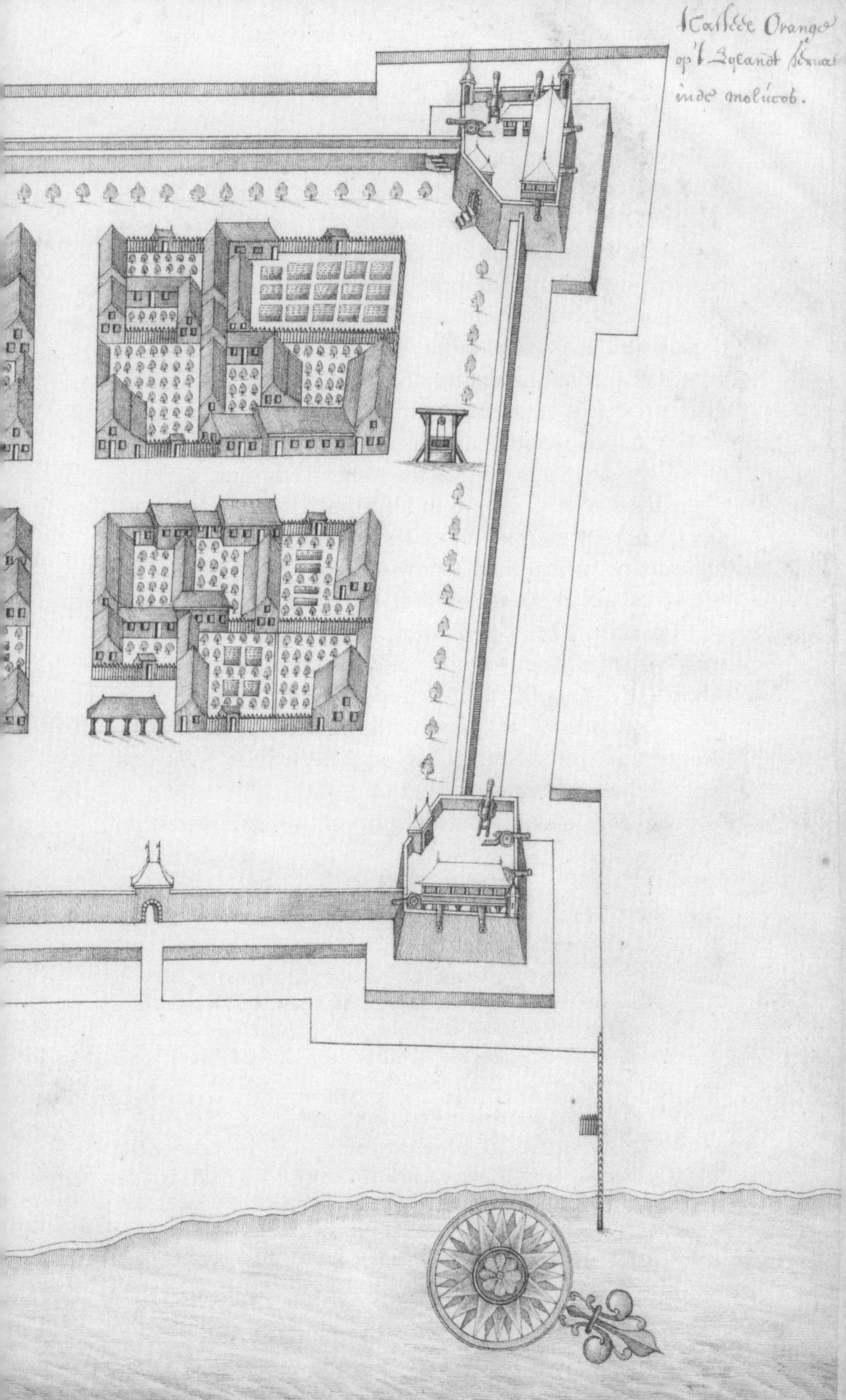
tCasteele Orange
op't Eylandt Ternaet
inde molucos.

the island of Nan'ao Dao, Matelieff's ships were escorted by vessels of the Imperial Ming navy to the Pearl River estuary. The Dutch ships dropped anchor off Lantau Island (now part of the Hong Kong SAR). Here, the admiral entered into negotiations with the authorities in Canton (Gangzhou). The Portuguese were determined to keep the Dutch out of China though and had spread rumors that they were a nation of pirates who could not be trusted. Realizing that his immediate prospects of opening direct trade with China were dim, Matelieff weighed anchor and sailed down the coast of present-day Vietnam and the Malay Peninsula, arriving at Banten[10] in western Java in December 1607. Matelieff set sail for Europe after taking on cargo and provisions for the homebound voyage and following face-to-face talks with his successor in Asia, Admiral Paul van Caerden[11], who was the third VOC fleet commander and had just arrived with his ships from Europe via Mozambique[12] and India. Aboard his flagship, Matelieff carried the emissaries of King Ekathotsarot of Siam to the Dutch Republic.[13] The fleet arrived in the Netherlands on 2 September, 1608, and Matelieff was celebrated as a hero.

So why should Matelieff be of special interest to

---

10   Port and polity in west Java near the Sunda Strait. See CMJ, 532; JDC, 352.

11   CMJ, 97-101. A travelogue recounting the voyage of Admiral Van Caerden was published as A. de Booy, ed., *De derde reis van de V.O.C. naar Oost-Indië onder het beleid van Admiraal Paulus van Caerden, uitgezeild in 1606*, 2 vols. (The Hague: Martinus Nijhoff, 1970).

12   See the list of place names (*Mozambique*).

13   CMJ, 46, 57; SMS, 93-4. See also Paul Pelliot, "Les Relations du Siam et de la Hollande en 1608," *T'oung Pao*, 32 (1936): 223-9; and J.J.L. Duyvendak, "The First Siamese Embassy to Holland," *T'oung Pao*, 32 (1936): 285-92; D. van der Cruysse, *Siam and the West, 1500-1700* (Chiang Mai: Silkworm Books, 2002), 43-50.

researchers of the Singapore-Johor nexus? Shortly after arriving home, Matelieff penned a series of epistolary memorials, or petitions, in which he provided a candid assessment of the VOC's state of affairs in the East Indies. In these, he spelled out what could be done to improve the operational efficiency and profitability of the Company. He carefully drew up a blueprint for the future of the Company in Asia, earning him the reputation among VOC historians today as a visionary of the first Dutch Empire.[14]

The memorials are evidence that Matelieff found the short-term horizon of ageing merchant directors to be a real impediment to the long-term strategic planning of the Company. In addition, he was aware that the success and survival of the VOC depended on fundamentally changing the way it conducted business, organized its voyages, optimized its departures from Europe, and governed its affairs in the East Indies. The admiral regarded it as pivotal that the Company balance its twin missions: on the one hand to conduct trade and generate income, and on the other, to fulfil its mandate from the government to extend the ongoing war of independence against Spain (and by extension Portugal) into the Asian theatre.[15] To this end, Matelieff recognized that the VOC would need to invest heavily in infrastructure in Asia and that such investments could not be achieved without direct government support. The admiral ensured that his memorials were circulated among the Dutch Republic's leading politicians of the day. In order to reach the highest members of government, Matelieff relied

---

14 See for example Femme S. Gaastra, *The Dutch East India Company. Expansion and Decline* (Zuphen: Walburg Pers, 2003), 39-40.

15 For a background to the war, its projection into Asia and its extension to the Portuguese, see CMJ, 6, 53-4; P. Borschberg, "From Self-Defense to an Instrument of War: Dutch Privateering Around the Malay Peninsula in the Early Seventeenth Century," *Journal of Early Modern History*, 17 (2013): 35-52.

Left: Portrait of Cornelis Matelieff de Jonge by Pieter van der Werff, c.1699. Amsterdam: Rijksmuseum, inv. SK-A-4491-00.

on the mediation of a young lawyer named Huig de Groot, better known today by his Latinized name Hugo Grotius. Later in life, Grotius would earn a reputation as being one of the foremost theorists of the laws of war and peace, as well as the law of nations.[16]

Though Matelieff relinquished his position on the VOC's central board of directors within months of his return to the Republic, he continued to serve as a member of the board of the Rotterdam Chamber for life. Matelieff also embarked on a political career that found its apex in serving as burgomaster, or mayor, of Rotterdam. In the latter years of his life, he travelled on business for longer periods to the Baltic Sea region, chiefly to Poland. Cornelis Matelieff de Jonge passed away in 1632 at the age of about 62.

The texts

Given this, which writings pertaining to the voyage of Admiral Matelieff should researchers focus on? And for someone specifically interested in the pre-1800 history of the Singapore-Johor nexus, what important insights can we learn?

The writings relating to Matelieff's voyage to the East Indies fall into two broad categories. The first is the *Journal* or travelogue; the second are his letters and memorials. In addition to these documents, there are also a number of testimonies written by third parties that support the Matelieff documents. Some of these, such as the letters of Ala'udin

---

16   Concerning Grotius in general, and specifically also his relationship to Matelieff, see: GPFT, 134-42; and more extensively in H.J.M. Nellen, *Hugo Grotius, A Lifelong Struggle for Peace in Church and State, 1583-1645* (Leiden: Brill, 2014), 205.

Ri'ayat Shah III[17] of Johor and Raja Bongsu to Stadholder[18] Prince Maurice of Nassau, or passages from the travelogue of Matelieff's successor in Johor, Admiral Pieter Willemsz. Verhoeff, have been added in English translation to this book.[19]

The *Journal* was not written and edited by Matelieff himself. It was evidently written by one or both of the men who served as Matelieff's personal secretaries during the voyage: initially Abraham van den Broeck and later Jacques l'Hermite de Jonge. Both men went on to do greater things: Van den Broeck was appointed head of the VOC factory[20] at Batu Sawar where he served from September 1606 to around March 1609, while l'Hermite was appointed to a senior position at the Company's Banten factory.

Though two shorter accounts of Matelieff's victory over the Portuguese viceroy's fleet off Melaka (penned by l'Hermite) circulated in the Dutch Republic within weeks of the admiral's return in early September 1608,[21] the far more

---

17   Ala'udin is also named Raja Mansur and Raja Rade in period sources.

18   Before the Dutch Revolt (1566/8-1648), the stadholder was the representative of the feudal overlord who was normally absent, a sort of governor-general. In the period of the Dutch Republic (after 1581) it emerged into the highest aristocratic office of state by its own right. See also CMJ, 516-7.

19   See documents 8 and 9 below.

20   This term refers in this instance to a fortified warehouse. See also the glossary (*factor, factory*).

21   See CMJ, 123-4, 126. The earlier or shorter text of the two was also translated into English at the time: "An historicall and true discourse, of a voyage made by the Admirall Cornelis Matelife the yonger, into the East Indies, who departed out of Holland, in May 1605: With the besieging of Malacca, and the battaile by him fought at sea against the Portugales in the Indies, with other discourses. Translated out of the Dutch, according to the coppie printed at Rotterdam, 1608" (Imprinted at London for William Barret, and are to be sold at his shop in

extensive travelogue or *Journal* was not published for some decades. It circulated in manuscript form among key members of government and the VOC. A sheet containing notes excerpted from the *Journal* is presently preserved in the collection of Grotius' working papers in the Dutch National Archives in The Hague.[22] The *Journal's* first edition only came several decades later, in 1645-6. It is found in the collection of early voyages, journals and travelogues compiled by Isaac Commelin.[23] A self-standing edition of the text followed in 1648—a full four decades after the actual events had taken place.[24]

Tucked away within the main text of the *Journal* are some materials of special interest to researchers of the Singapore-Johor region. This includes full transcripts of letters written by King Ala'udin and Raja Bongsu of Johor, as well as treaties concluded between Matelieff and the Johor rulers, all translated into Dutch. A close reading of the *Journal* further reveals echoes of conversations touching on

---

Paules Church-yard, at the signe of the greene Dragon, 1608). For a copy of this translation, see CMJ, 401-20.

22   The Hague, National Archives, *Collectie Hugo de Groot*, Supplement (access code 1.35.10.02, no. 40), fol. 403 recto. An image of this sheet is also reproduced in CMJ, 155.

23   Isaac Commelin, *Begin ende Voortgang Vande Vereenigde Neerlandsche Geoctroyeerde Oost-Indische Compagnie*, 4 vols., facsimile reproduction of the original printed in Amsterdam in 1646 in 2 vols. (Amsterdam: Facsimile Uitgaven Nederland, 1969). Matelieff's voyage is contained in vol. 3 of the facsimile edition and features a separate pagination numbering.

24   *Journael Ende Historische Verhael/ van de treffelijcke Reyse/ gedaen naer Oost-Indien, ende China, met elf Schepen, Door den Manhaften Admirael Cornelis Matelieff de Jonge. Uyt-ghevaren in den Jare 1605. En wat haer in de volgende Jaren 1606, 1607, ende 1608 weder-varen is. Een seer Vreemde en Wonderlijcke Reyse* (t' Amstelredam, Door Joost Hartgers, Boeck-verkooper in de Gasthuys-Steegh, bezijden het Stadt-huys, in de Boeck-winckel, 1648).

the negotiations for the two Johor-Dutch treaties of May and September 1606. On the basis of these documents, it transpires that the Johor rulers were exercising agency in giving the final shape and form to these documents and drove a hard bargain when they felt that their interests were not being sufficiently safeguarded.

The letters and memorials form a separate category of writings because they contained sensitive political and commercial information that was not intended reading for a larger audience. Which document represents a memorial and which a letter is not always sufficiently clear, especially since the memorials are generally written as letters.

With exceptions, the most important letters and memorials have survived through the centuries in a common source: the former working papers of Hugo Grotius. His notes and manuscripts remained intact as a family possession until 1864 when they were sold off at a public auction organized by Martinus Nijhoff in The Hague.[25] The Rijksarchief, the predecessor of the National Archives of the Netherlands, was the successful bidder of several manuscripts sold on this occasion, including some of the letters and memorials by Matelieff. Other successful bidders for Matelieff's letters and memorials include, notably, the Municipal Archives in Rotterdam as well as the private collector and Amsterdam-based bookseller Frederik Muller.[26] A subsequent auction of

---

25 *Catalogue des Manuscrits Autographes de Hugo Grotius. Vente à La Haye, 15 Novembre 1864, sous la direction et au domicile de Martinus Nijhoff* (The Hague: Martinus Nijhoff, 1864) as well as L.J. Noordhoff, *Beschrijving van het zich in Nederland bevindende en nog onbeschreven gedeelte der papieren afkomstig van Huig de Groot welke in 1864 te 's-Gravenhage zijn geveild* (Groningen-Djakarta: Noordhoff, 1953); also R. Bijlsma, "De discoursen van Cornelis Matelieff de Jonge over den Staat van Oost-Indië," *Nederlandsch Archievenblad* 35 (1927-8): 49-53. See also GPFT, 3-4.

26 See CMJ, 52, 101n401.

the latter's private collection some years later brought more of Matelieff's writings into the possession of the Rijksarchief. Matelieff's manuscripts in the Dutch National Archives are preserved today in a bundle consisting mainly of unpublished manuscripts and titled *Collectie Hugo de Groot, Supplement* (Hugo Grotius Collection, Supplement).[27] From his correspondence and personal notes, we know that Grotius had passed the memorials to the Land's Advocate of Holland, Johan van Oldenbarnevelt, a senior statesman of the Dutch Republic who held a position broadly comparable today with the Speaker of the House and Prime Minister.[28] Grotius was a known protégé of Oldenbarnevelt, and the young man certainly had the statesman's attention. Grotius had been chosen to pass some of Matelieff's memorials to Oldenbarnevelt and this young prodigy did what most of us would do if placed in such a position: he arranged to have copies made by his secretary. For this reason, many of the items found in the former working papers of Grotius are secretarial copies, and the signed originals can sometimes be found among the working papers of Oldenbarnevelt. These are preserved in a separate collection now deposited in the Dutch National Archives.[29]

Although the public sale of Grotius' papers had stirred considerable interest within academic, legal and diplomatic circles, the focus of this interest was squarely placed on Grotius' own drafts and notes relating to the laws of war and peace. The star among those papers was, without a shade

---

27 The Hague, National Archives, *Collectie Hugo de Groot Supplement*, access code 1.10.35.02, no. 40.

28 For a brief outline of the powers exercised by the Land's Advocate, see CMJ, 492. Concerning the life and works of this important pioneer statesman of the Dutch Republic, see Jan den Tex, *Oldenbarnevelt*, 2 vols. (Cambridge: Cambridge University Press, 1974).

29 The Hague, National Archives, *Collectie Johan van Oldenbarnevelt*, access code 3.01.14.

of doubt, the Latin manuscript known today as the *Law of Prize and Booty* (*De Jure Praedae*).[30] At the time the papers were prepared for auction, this piece had been regarded as an early draft of Grotius' landmark work *Three Books on the Law of War and Peace* (*De Jure Belli ac Pacis Libri Tres*).[31] However on closer reading, the manuscript was discovered to be an early exposé on the laws of war in its own right, written and revised over several years as part of a commission Grotius had received from the VOC around October 1604. Only one of its chapters was published in Grotius' own lifetime; it bears the title *The Free Sea* (*Mare Liberum*) and was a booklet rushed through to press in late 1608 and early 1609. This was around the time Matelieff had returned from his voyage to the East Indies and when the Twelve Years Truce[32] was in the final stages of negotiation.[33]

The excitement surrounding the discovery of *The Law of Prize and Booty* and its first publication in 1868 drowned out another key set of sources found among the working papers of Grotius: the memorials and letters of Admiral Matelieff. In the volume of the *Rotterdamsche Historiebladen* (*Rotterdam History Papers*) published in 1867, J.G. Frederiks penned the first modern biography of Matelieff to which he appended transcripts of letters and memorials, most

---

30   For an English translation, see H. Grotius, De Jure Praedae Commentarius. *Commentary on the Law of Prize and Booty. A Translation of the Original Manuscript of 1604*, trans. G.L. Williams and W.H. Zeydel (Oxford: Clarendon Press, 1950).

31   For an English translation, see H. Grotius, *De Jure Belli ac Pacis*, trans. F.W. Kelsey, ed. J.B. Scott, reprint of the original edition of 1925 (New York: Oceana Publications, 1964).

32   A ceasefire or truce (1609-21) between the Dutch Republic and the Spanish and Portuguese Empires.

33   Concerning the historical background to this work, see GPFT, 30. For an English translation, see H. Grotius, *The Free Sea*, trans. Richard Hakluyt, ed. and intr. D. Armitage (Indianapolis: Liberty Fund, 2004).

of which had been found among Grotius' former working papers.[34] While the aim of this publication was to render the papers of Matelieff more accessible to the general public, the mid-19th century edition by Frederiks remains problematic: apart from the many transcription errors, he published the texts without annotation. This publication, moreover, is not easily found, not even in the Netherlands. Not surprising then, until now, these important documents have had that minimal reach beyond a handful of VOC historians based in the Netherlands.

Singapore

So what can someone interested in the pre-1800 history of the Singapore-Johor nexus glean from these materials connected to Matelieff?

The documents, taken in conjunction with some additional supporting materials relating to the voyage of the fifth VOC fleet commander, Pieter Willemsz. Verhoeff, offer a fairly rich source of information on the region. Admittedly, they do not contain the detailed observations of Matelieff's contemporary Jacques de Coutre,[35] but they are no less interesting.

The single most important statement about Singapore concerns its *shahbandar*, or port master. The *Journal* records that on arriving off the coast of Melaka, two vessels from Johor approached the Dutch fleet. The text recounts:[36]

"Toward the evening, two *perahus* from Johor

---

34 J.G. Frederiks, "Cornelis Cornelisz Matelieff de Jonge en zijn geslagt," *Rotterdamsche Historiebladen*, J.H. Scheffer and Fr. D.O. Obreen, ed., 3 afd., 1.1 (1871): 204-357.

35 See esp. P. Borschberg, ed., *Jacques de Coutre's Singapore and Johor* (Singapore: NUS Press, 2015).

36 CMJ, 150-1.

joined the fleet ... The commander was the *shah-bandar* of Singapore, called Sri Raja Negara. Admiral [Matelieff] welcomed them as they were coming from the king of Johor, our ally, and let them navigate through the fleet and view the ships. They told him that the king had sent them to see if there were ships from Holland, because he had received a message from Perak that some ships had sailed to Melaka which were thought to be Dutch."

Let us examine this passage more closely: Singapore had a shahbandar or port master—which implies that Singapore still had a functioning port in 1606. Admittedly, we do not know how big or how busy this port was at the time, but it must have been significant enough to warrant the presence of a shahbandar. The *Journal* confirms here what we know from other period sources, notably the autobiography of Jacques de Coutre.[37] The settlement *Shabandaria*[38] is evidently named after the residence or compound of this official. Maps drawn around the same time by the Eurasian cartographer Manuel Godinho de Erédia confirm this name (the latter wrote the name *Shahbandaria* with the letter "X"— *Xabandaria*—in conformity with conventions of pronunciation and spelling in Portuguese of that period.[39]) Where this shahbandar's compound in Singapore was located is not certain: some have surmised it might have been around where the *temenggong*[40] later resided in the early 19th cen-

---

37   JCSJ, 15, 24.

38   See the list of place names (*Shahbandaria*).

39   See the redrawn map, 27.

40   A high-ranking Malay official in charge of security, prisons and customs. According to the *Undang-undang Melaka* (Laws of Melaka), the temenggong (the title has been translated into English as "police chief") was given "jurisdiction over crimes committed in the country [*di dalam negeri*] and (matters) such as the investigation (of crime) and the apprehension of crim-

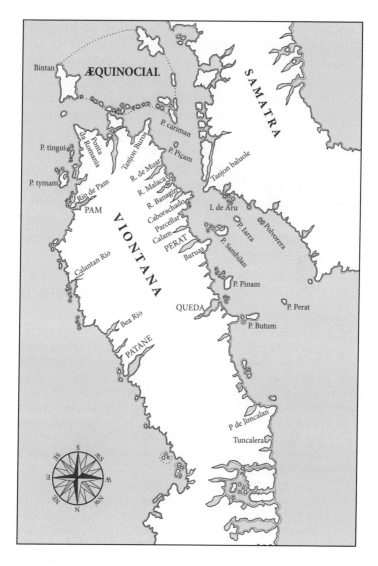

*Hand-drawn map of the Malay Peninsula and Sumatra by Man-
uel Godinho de Erédia (redrawn by Ms. Lee Li Kheng, GIS Map
and Resource United, National University of Singapore). The
original is found in Erédia's Declaraçam de Malaca (Description
of Melaka), c.1613.*

tury, namely near Raffles' Landing Place along the Singapore River. More likely however, it was located further to the east around the Kallang River estuary, perhaps a predecessor settlement at, or near, present-day Kampung Glam. Bear in mind that the shahbandar is a high-ranking Malay official. In the tradition of the *Undang-undang Melaka* (Laws of Melaka) that trace their origin to the time of the Melaka sultanate (15th-early 16th centuries), the shahbandar's authority was essentially one of a mediator between the foreign merchants and the royalty. He had such a dominant position over the foreign traders that the *Undang-undang Melaka* dubbed him the "father and mother of foreign merchants".[41] As was the case in the time of the Melaka sultanate, shahbandars were often of foreign origin and frequently managed the assets of the ruler and his immediate family. They also supervised imports and warehousing (in

---

inals in the land [*di dalam negeri*]." According to Tomé Pires, *The Suma Oriental of Tome Pires. An Account of the East from the Red Sea to Japan. Written in Malacca and India in 1512-1515*, ed. Armando Cortesão, 2 vols. (London: Hakluyt Society, 1944), II, 265, "He has charge of the guard and has many people under his jurisdiction. All prison cases go first to him and from him to the [bendahara], and this office always falls to persons of great esteem. He is also the one who receives the dues on the merchandise."

41   UUM, 123; also 62-3. Concerning the powers of the shahbandar in general, see also BOC, III, 593; EFS, II, 1409; GLA, II, 419-20; GVOC, 69, 106; HJ, 816; JDC, 342-3; Pires, *Suma Oriental*, II, 265; H. Dunlop, ed., *Bronnen tot de Geschiedenis der Oostindische Compagnie in Perzië, eerste deel, 1611-1638* (The Hague: Martinus Nijhoff, 1930), 795; P.G. Leupe, "The Siege and Capture of Malacca from the Portuguese in 1640-1641. Extracts from the Archives of the Dutch East India Company," trans. Mac Hacobian, *JMBRAS*, 14.1 (1936): 126; Muhammad Yusof Hashim, *The Malay Sultanate of Malacca*, trans. D.J. Muzaffar Tate (Kuala Lumpur: Dewan Bahasa dan Pustaka, 1992), 138.

his compound?) of imports, either brought in directly on ships owned by the ruler and his family, or goods purchased from foreign merchants. Now if Singapore was significant enough to warrant the presence of a shahbandar—an official with all those considerable responsibilities—surely we can conclude that Singapore was not a neglected backwater since around 1400, as 19th and early 20th century British sources have led us to believe.

Let us now return to the original passage found in Matelieff's *Journal* and examine its choice of terminology a bit more closely. Here it is claimed that this official from Singapore was also known as Sri Raja Negara. So it would appear that the shahbandar held a double title or function: he was the shahbandar and was known concurrently as the Raja Negara. What do we know about this latter position?

From the Malay-Bugis chronicle *Tuhfat-al-Nafis* (*The Precious Gift*) dating from the second half of the 19th century, the Raja Negara was also known as the *Raja Negara Selat* or also *ketua orang laut*. He was therefore the head of the *orang laut* community in the Straits region. Some authors have further associated this title with the *hulubalang besar*, a titular honorific known from an era when Singapore fell under the rule of the Melaka sultanate.[42] Carl Otto Blagden notes that the title implied an essentially military function

---

42   Ali al-Haji ibn Ahmad, *The Precious Gift/ Tuhfat al-Nafis*, ed. and trans. V.M. Hooker and Barbara Watson Andaya (Kuala Lumpur and New York: Oxford University Press, 1982). See also Borschberg, "The Seizure of the Sta. Catarina Revisited," *JSEAS*, 33.1 (2002): 59-60, esp. note 134, and Kwa Chong Guan, "Records and Notices of Early Singapore," in *Archeological Research on the "Forbidden Hill" in Singapore. Excavations at Fort Canning*, ed. John N. Miksic, (Singapore: National Museum, 1984) 121, "... Seri Raja Nugara, a title awarded, according to a later (Shellebear) edition of the *Sejarah Melayu*, to the Datin of Singapura, an acknowledged *hulubalang* of the sultan of Johor."

21

of captain or local military chief, and the title was sometimes also extended to local rulers.[43] The hulubalang besar of Singapore—as Muhammad Yusof Hashim explains—was specifically associated with the leadership of the nomadic sea tribes, the orang laut.[44] And who were the orang laut in the early 17th century? They acted as the naval forces to the Johor rulers.[45] In sum, the shahbandar of Singapore was also the head of the orang laut communities who in turn served aboard the armada of the Johor rulers.

These deliberations now lead us to another section of Matelieff's *Journal*, namely the description of the four surviving sons of the late Raja Ali Jalla bin Abdul Jalil who is said to have passed away around the year 1597.[46] One of the four sons is referred to as the *Raja Laut*—which may very

---

43   C.O. Blagden, ed., and M.J. Bremmer, trans., "Report of Governor Balthasar Bort on Malacca, 1678," *JMBRAS*, 5.1 (1927): 1-232, esp. 222.

44   Muhammad Yusof Hashim, *The Malay Sultanate of Malacca*, 109, 217.

45   According to Pires, the orang laut did so only for food and without remuneration. Pires, *Suma Oriental*, II, 264. See M.A.P. Meilink-Roelofsz, *Asian Trade and European Influence in the Indonesian Archipelago between 1500 and about 1630* (The Hague: Martinus Nijhoff, 1962), 29, and Manuel Lobato, "Melaka is like a cropping field," *Journal of Asian History*, 46.2 (2012): 230.

46   Pinto, "Captains, Sultans and liaisons dangereuses: Melaka and Johor in the Late Sixteenth Century," in *Iberians in the Singapore-Melaka Area and Adjacent Regions*, ed. Peter Borschberg (Wiesbaden and Lisbon: Harrassowitz and Fundação Oriente, 2009), 143, 145. Concerning the year of Raja Ali's passing, see M. Godinho de Erédia, "Informação da Aurea Chersoneso," in *Ordenações da Índia do Senhor Rei D. Manoel, etc.*, ed. A.L. Caminha (Lisbon: Na Impressão Regia, 1807), 70; and *M. Godinho de Erédia, Informação da Aurea Quersoneso, ou Península, e das Ilhas Auríferas, Carbúculas e Aromáticas*, ed. R.M. Loureiro (Macau: Centro Científico e Cultural de Macau, 2008), 71.

well be a rendition of Sri Raja Negara's honorifics. In sharp contrast to Raja Bongsu (alias Raja Seberang or Raja di Ilir),[47] whom Matelieff found to be competent and trustworthy, the *Journal* had nothing but scorn for his half-brother, Raja Laut: [48]

"From his third wife, [Raja Ali Jalla], the old king of Johor, had a son named Raja Laut that is 'king of the sea'—a man capable of nothing but smoking tobacco, drinking arak and chewing betel with it, indeed worthy of being bound hands and feet and sunk into the sea; a big drunkard, killer and fornicator, and everything to do with those three things he knows inside out."

Since we have already established that the shahbandar and the Raja Negara Selat (or Raja Laut) are the same individual, might he also be the *laksamana* or admiral of Johor? There are several reasons to draw this conclusion. First, as Muhammad Yusof has already established, the office of the laksamana during the Melaka Sultanate traced its origins to the hulubalang besar of Singapore—that is to the chief of the orang laut communities.[49] We also know from the *Commentaries of Alfonso de Albuquerque*, published around the middle of the 16th century, that the laksamana had settled in Singapore following the Portuguese takeover of Melaka in 1511.[50] This may very well have also been around

---

47   See the glossary (*Raja Bongsu*).

48   CMJ, 154.

49   Muhammad Yusof Hashim, *The Malay Sultanate of Melaka,*109, 217.

50   B. de Albuquerque, *Comentarios de Afonso d'Albuqerque*, J. Veríssimo Serrão, ed. and int., text of the 2nd edition of 1576, 2 vols. (Lisbon: Imprensa Nacional-Casa de Moeda, 1973); *Commentaries of the Great Afonso Dalboquerque, Second Viceroy of India, W. de Gray Birch*, ed. and trans., 4 vols. (London: Hakluyt Society, 1880).

the time when the fugitive Melaka sultan is said to have lived on the island, as is reported in the letter of Alfonso de Albuquerque dated 22 February, 1513, as well as later by the VOC historian Pieter van Dam at the turn of the 17th and 18th centuries.[51] In this light, one can therefore say that the Melaka laksamana returned to his home base in Singapore during the early 16th century, and that his descendants on the island remained there until Matelieff arrived almost a century later.

So what are the functions of a laksamana? First and foremost, he is a commander at sea, an admiral. The *Undang-undang Melaka* describes the laksamana as the *Raja Laut*—the "king of the sea".[52] He is one of the highest ranking nobles, standing fourth in precedence after the *bendahara* (first minister).[53] As in the period of the Melaka sultanate, the laksamana was placed in charge of protocol and the reception of foreign embassies. In close consultation with the ruler, the bendahara and also the temenggong, he actively participated in policy decisions.[54] The laksamana's other functions sometimes shadowed those of the shahbandar or the bendahara: he exercised certain rights over foreign merchants and was normally heavily involved in trade.

All this tells us something about the state of Singapore at the beginning of the 17th century. This would have been

---

51 A. de Albuquerque, *Cartas de Afonso de Albuquerque*, ed. Raymundo A. de Bulhão Pato et al., 7 vols. (Lisbon: Academia das Ciências Morais, Políticas e Belas-Artes, 1884-1935), III, 58 (letter of 22 February, 1513); P. van Dam, *Beschryvinge van de Oostindische Compagnie*, ed. F.W. Stapel, 8. vols. (The Hague: Martinus Nijhoff, 1931), vol. II.1, 327.

52 Muhammad Yusof Hashim, *The Malay Sultanate of Melaka*, 134-7.

53 See also the glossary (*Bendahara*).

54 Pires, *Suma Oriental*, II, 264, "... but first of all [the bendahara] informs the king, and both decide the matter in consultation with the [laksamana] and the [temenggong]."

home to not just the residence of the shahbandar, but also of his warehouses, agents and support staff (slaves). This shahbandar of Singapore was also the head of the orang laut communities in and around the Straits—and these orang laut served as rowers and soldiers aboard the galleys of the Johor rulers. In view of this royal title, together with its deep historical connections to the hulubalang besar, it would also suggest that the shahbandar concurrently held the title of laksamana. The Dutch academic Pieter Gerritsz. Rouffaer came to this same conclusion in a study published in 1921,[55] but that is by no means conclusive. There is one small piece of evidence against this association of the Raja Laut with the laksamana or admiral: in one of his memorials, Matelieff claims that the temenggong was the "admiral", and this admiral, it is further said, was an intelligent man quite unlike the personal qualities associated with Raja Laut. But this short statement from the *Journal* is all we have to go by, and it is also the one and only reference that Matelieff made to the temenggong of Johor.

Whether acting as a shahbandar or laksamana or possibly both, this is certainly one of the key reasons why, in 1606, the king of Johor dispatched the Singapore-based official on a five-day trip to Melaka to ascertain with his own eyes that the Dutch fleet had arrived from Europe. All this points to one important conclusion: Singapore could have hardly been a backwater in 1606. On the contrary, it had a functioning port and must have been one of the principal bases—if not *the* principal base—of Johor's armada at the time.

---

55   RWME: 488n1; also GPFT, 366n85.

25

Clash of civilizations?

When the shahbandar of Singapore returned to his king to inform him that the Dutch fleet had arrived, more oared galleys were dispatched to meet Matelieff's ships off Melaka. The *Journal* offers a record of the negotiations that took place aboard Matelieff's flagship between the admiral and Raja Bongsu. These negotiations hammered out the conditions of the first formal Dutch-Johor alliance and for the division of spoils should the joint military campaign succeed in wresting Melaka from the Portuguese. The exchange of words was almost certainly recorded by Abraham van den Broeck who served as Matelieff's personal secretary at the time.[56] This record stands out for its candidness, honesty, and evident willingness by the Dutch to learn and understand their treaty partners. It offers a sharp contrast to similar documents from the British dating from the 19th and even early 20th centuries which generally regard the Malay rulers as passive, backward, and reluctant respondents to European initiatives.[57] This is most definitely not the picture

---

56 CMJ, 236, above, p. 12, and below p. 139, 167.
57 See broadly John Legge, "The Writing of Southeast Asian History," in *The Cambridge History of Southeast Asia*, ed. N. Tarling, 2 vols. (Cambridge: Cambridge University Press, 1992), I, 1-50; Anthony Milner, "Colonial Records History: British Malaya," *Modern Asian Studies*, 21.4 (1987): 773-92; J.R.W. Smail, "On the Possibility of an Autonomous History of Modern Southeast Asia," *Journal of Southeast Asian History*, 2 (1961): 72-102; Harry J. Benda, "The Structure of Southeast Asian History: Some Preliminary Observations," *JSEAH* 3.1 (1962): 106-38; Ariel Heryanto, "Can there be Southeast Asians in Southeast Asian Studies?," in *Knowing Southeast Asian Subjects*, ed. Laurie J. Sears (Seattle and Singapore: University of Washington Press and NUS Press, 2007), 75-108, esp. what he has to say on agency, p. 97-8. See also the introduction by Hans Hägerdal, *Responding to the West: Essays on Colonial Domination and Asian Agency* (Amsterdam: Amsterdam University Press, 2009), 9-16.

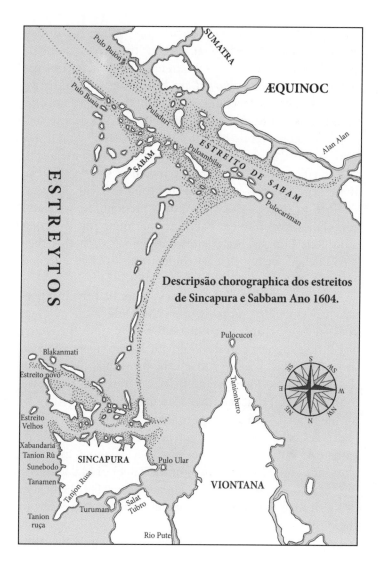

Hand-drawn map of Singapore and the surrounding straits by Manuel Godinho de Erédia (redrawn by Ms. Lee Li Kheng, GIS and Map Resource Unit, National University of Singapore). The original is found in Erédia's Declaraçam de Malaca (Description of Melaka), c.1613, fol. 61 recto.

being painted in Matelieff's documents. While the British later became frustrated by rajas whom they accused of hiding behind courtly ritual and religion, the royal personages in Van den Broeck's *Journal* are brimming with initiative and agency: it was Raja Bongsu who sent the first formal diplomatic mission to the Dutch Republic in 1603, whose surviving members returned with Matelieff's fleet.[58] And it was Johor that had suggested a joint campaign against Melaka to rid the city and the surrounding region of the Portuguese. These negotiations—and those that followed with Admiral Verhoeff in 1609[59]—show how astute the Johorese were and how they drove a tough bargain. The Johor royals—especially Raja Bongsu—were shrewd diplomats. Whether they left Matelieff feeling that he could wage war and do good business with them is a different question.

A close reading of the sources shows that the two parties had difficulty properly understanding each another. That's not surprising, for at that moment in time, the Dutch had little experience in dealing with Malay rulers and vice versa. The VOC was very much the proverbial new boy on the block whose identity and behavior were still unknown to the local rulers at the time. Captured in the negotiations for the Johor-Dutch alliance are some deep running cultural fault lines between the two parties. Admittedly, the insights gained do not actually reveal novel facets about the inner workings of the Johor court or of the values of Malay rulers, but they do support things we already know. For the benefit of the reader, I will briefly single out and explain a few of these cultural fault lines.

The first, and probably the most striking, is the comparatively high value placed on human life by the Southeast Asian rulers in comparison to their Dutch guests. Mass slaughter on the battlefield was evidently not the Malay

---

58   CMJ, 54, and also below p. 79, 91.

59   See documents 8 and 9.

manner of waging war. As Matelieff's contemporary Manuel Godinho de Erédia explained: "The armed forces of the [Malays] do not follow the ordered military tactics of Europe … Their sole plan is to construct an ambush in the narrow paths and woods and thickets, and then make an attack with a body of armed men. Whenever they draw themselves up for battle, they acquit themselves badly and usually suffer heavy losses."[60] This helps explain a few things: the manifest reluctance of the Johorese *orang kaya*[61] to sacrifice the lives of their slaves in fighting the Portuguese; the lack of enthusiasm on the part of the Johorese to engage the Portuguese in hand-to-hand combat; and the practice of capturing alive those who sought to flee from Melaka. As for the reluctance by the orang kaya to send their slaves into battle, the *Journal* explains: "… they all feared to lose their slaves, who are their only riches."[62] In other words, wealth in Johor was measured not by money, but by the labor over which one could command.

This comparatively high value placed on human life contrasts with the low value placed on land. This is no minor issue. The Dutch Republic—and especially the coastal provinces of Holland and Zeeland—were (and still are) heavily populated regions where land was very valuable. In the 17th century Dutch Republic, the cost of living and the level of wealth was high, and so was the price of land. This contrasts with the sparsely populated regions of the Malay Peninsula. One should therefore not be surprised by the sense of bewilderment arising from the following two passages taken from the *Journal*. The first stems from the negotiations in May 1606 between Matelieff and Raja Bongsu for the spoils of war; the second from a description of Batu Sawar made later

---

60   MGED, 31.

61   See the glossary (*orang kaya*).

62   CMJ, 166, and also p. 104.

that year during the month of September: [63]

> "After long protestations as to who would make his demand first, Admiral [Matelieff] even had to give in to [Raja Bongsu] and make his demand, stating that he wanted the city to conduct trade and store his goods, and to occupy it with Dutch. The king was to have all of the country [outside the city], and they would help each other like brothers against all enemies in defensive [war] and against the Portuguese and Spanish in offensive war. To this the king replied that if he was not to have the city, why would he want to take it from the hands of the Portuguese? As to the countryside, he did not care, he had 20 times more land than he could fill with subjects. Furthermore, this could not be called help, but merely a change from a worse to a better situation, and even that could turn out differently over time if our people were like the Portuguese, something he could not be certain of. In that case, it could not be said that we came to his aid, but that he came to ours, to give his own land to a party more unknown than the one who had it now, merely in the hope of better neighborliness.

> … All the land belongs to the king and is hardly valued, so that whoever asks it of him can receive enough land. It appears to be very fertile nonetheless, for it is full of trees and the grass reaches up to a man's belly. But the land is not cultivated, for if they turned to agriculture they would have everything in abundance, whereas now they are in want of many things."[64]

To a Dutchman of the 17th century, it must have

---

63   CMJ, 156 and below, pp. 96-7.
64   CMJ, 191-2, and below, p. 109.

seemed quite outlandish to hear a ruler say that he "did not care about land", to learn that land was virtually worthless, and that anyone who asked the ruler could "receive enough land".[65] Moreover, the request by the Dutch to lay down in writing a right to "fetch and cut wood from the king's land" must have seemed equally strange to Raja Bongsu. But we must remember: wood was always expensive in the Netherlands, and lumber was especially expensive in the first half of 17th century during the so-called Little Ice Age (c.1550-1850) when some of the lowest average temperatures prevailed in Europe. Most people would have cooked and heated their homes with wood, and anyone who owned woodland in northern Europe at the time had a real money spinner.

A Dutch fort for Singapore

Let us now return to the negotiations between Admiral Matelieff and Raja Bongsu aboard the Dutch flagship for a joint military campaign against Melaka. What resulted from these talks was a treaty ratified and sworn on 17 May, 1606. As the unfolding events would have it, however, Melaka could not be wrested from the Portuguese in the course of the ensuing weeks and months. In September, Matelieff withdrew his ships to the Johor River in order to make urgent repairs to his vessels. On this occasion, he also visited the Johor royal court at Batu Sawar. We will be examining his observations on Batu Sawar made on this occasion a little later in this introduction, but for now, suffice it to say that the time for a new agreement with Johor had come. The May 1606 treaty concerned itself mainly with the arrangements that would kick in should Melaka be successfully taken by the Dutch and their Johorese allies. As this did not come to

---

65   CMJ, 191-2, and also below, p. 109.

Left: Portrait of Pieter Willemsz. Verhoeff, (artist unknown), c.1607. Rijksmuseum Amsterdam M-SK-A-1469-00.

pass, an alternative (transitional) arrangement was hammered out until another military campaign was possible—and successful. The second treaty of Johor, ratified on 23 September, 1606, confirmed the earlier arrangements made in May but one important additional clause was added with this new document: it provided for "a secure and permanent place for [Dutch] subjects to further their trade in the East Indies."[66] In other words, a place where they could gather and store their goods, equipment and ammunition and make repairs to their vessels. The treaty enabled the Dutch to build houses and bring in craftsmen and settlers as they would have been able to do had Melaka been successfully plucked from the Portuguese. To this end, the king of Johor committed himself to grant the Dutch a plot of land "as big or small" as the Dutch would seem fit for the purpose, either on the mainland and the Johor River, or alternatively on one of the islands "under His Majesty's authority".[67] The wording was sufficiently vague to cover different scenarios, depending on how the Dutch might interpret them in the future. A taste of this came with the next Dutch admiral to visit Batu Sawar after Matelieff. This was Pieter Willemsz. Verhoeff who arrived during the first weeks of 1609.

After ascertaining that a joint attack on Portuguese Melaka was neither feasible nor likely to be successful, Verhoeff followed his instructions from the Gentlemen Directors and sought to revise the Matelieff treaty of September 1606.[68] Supported by his broad council,[69] the

---

66   CMJ, 158, under article 2; and below, p. 111.

67   CMJ, 398 and below, p. 112.

68   See documents 8 and 9.

69   The broad council (*brede raad*) fulfilled the function as both an advisory and decision-making body on important com-

admiral proposed the construction of a Dutch fortification in Johor. Raja Bongsu was dismayed. He claimed that his Malay-language copy of the treaty said nothing of a fortification, only of a secure place on which to build warehouses, store goods, and bring in craftsmen.[70] His version of the treaty, the raja insisted, said nothing of a Dutch fort.[71] The Johorese clearly had serious doubts about this scheme: officially they were worried that the Dutchmen would chase after and deflower Johorese women,[72] and while that was doubtlessly a genuine concern, the real reasons were certainly more complex, and were chiefly security related. On another occasion, Raja Bongsu explained that he was unsure whether one should give the Dutch the "keys to his river", and in any case, he had no power to do so on his own accord.[73] The Dutch fortification, planned for the region around the Johor River estuary or the Singapore Straits between Karimun[74] and Bintan, could possibly place a stranglehold on the upstream towns, including the commercially active capital Batu Sawar. Why would the Raja want to let some party of strangers control maritime traffic through the straits and on his principal river? After all, the Dutch were relative newcomers compared to the Portuguese, and who was to say that the Dutch would not eventually behave like the Portuguese sometime in the future?[75]

---

mercial and military issues. It was also responsible for adjudicating offences committed aboard vessels. The broad council was composed of leading naval officers of the fleet (usually the commanders of each vessel of the fleet) as well as senior commercial officers.

70   CMJ, 398 and below, p. 111.

71   See below, p. 193.

72   SMS, 125.

73   SMS, 130.

74   See the list of place names (*Karimun*).

75   CMJ, 156, 195.

If Raja Bongsu and other leading members of the Johor royal court had become suspicious of the Dutch and their long-term intentions, feelings now spilled over into outright anger and disappointment. It was bad enough that they were unable to expel the Portuguese from Melaka in a military campaign. But could they not take on another one of Johor's other long-standing enemies: Patani? To this effect, King Ala'udin and Raja Bongsu even penned a letter to the king of Holland,[76] explaining the background to their conflict as well as the dishonor that had been done to their brother by the ruler of Patani. That campaign, however, was for another day, and Verhoeff raised anchor and set sail from the Johor River. A new low point was attained later that year: news reached the Johor royal court that the Dutch had entered into negotiations with the king of Spain and Portugal for a truce. To the Johorese royals, this was a clear and open breach of the treaty they had signed with Matelieff in May 1606: Article 10 unambiguously stated that "Neither party will have the power to make peace with the king of Spain without both parties' consent."[77] The Dutch had moved on this truce[78] without seeking consent of their Johor ally—and Raja Bongsu, again, penned a letter of complaint to the king of Holland on 8 December, 1609.[79] Why was Johor not being treated as an equal? Why was each new visiting Dutch admiral seeking to tinker with the original treaty signed with Matelieff? This was clearly unacceptable to the Johor rulers.

We know that these letters of complaint from the Johor court were received in the Dutch Republic and found their

---

76   This is a term coined already in the early years of the VOC to refer to the States General and sometimes also the Stadholder(s) of the Dutch Republic. See also the glossary (*King of Holland*).

77   CMJ, 159; and below, p. 101.

78   That is the Twelve Years Truce.

79   CMJ, 441-5; and and document 11.

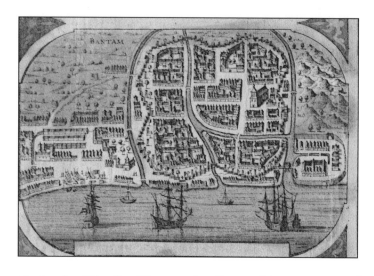

Cartouche of the city of Banten taken from a 17th century map of Southeast Asia. Peter Borschberg, private collection.

intended recipients. It would also appear that Matelieff had read them. To the admiral, this was the sad outcome of the way the fleet commander system of the VOC worked in practice: each fleet admiral was a plenipotentiary, but often inexperienced in the ways of handling Asian rulers. Experience had shown that the fleet commanders had a propensity to tread on each other's toes, and undo what another had achieved by careful negotiation. There can be little doubt that Matelieff had the case of Johor in mind here, and it certainly did not help that he did not hold Verhoeff's diplomatic skills in high esteem. But the damage had already been done. In his memorial of 31 August, 1610, passed to Grotius, Matelieff wrote:[80]

> "... The Gentlemen Directors have been informed with the latest arriving ships that the king of Johor

---

80   CMJ, 346; and below, pp. 154-5.

is completely opposed to creating a fortress in his country, so that need will make us understand what we cannot understand by reason. .... [The king of Johor] ... does not want to concede us a fortress there, as I and Pieter Willemsz. [Verhoeff] after me have found out by experience."

Surviving materials prove that the Dutch were at a loss as to how to handle the politically delicate situation in Johor. Already before Verhoeff's diplomatic faux-pas at Batu Sawar, Dutch ships had generally bypassed Johor for business and called at Patani instead. Matelieff explained in August 1610:[81]

"The king of Johor, who is our friend, is being reduced to misery because of our friendship; and what is more, the pepper which his land produces is transported to Patani and bought at a higher price by us there than in Johor. Thus we deprive him of trade while we ought to do the contrary, and we drive the trade toward the people of Patani, who have none themselves and who make us pay as much toll as they want to."

Relations with Johor were sensitive, and no one knew that more than the VOC's man-on-the-spot, Jacques Obelaer. Obelaer's team had taken over from Abraham van den Broeck around the time that Admiral Verhoeff sailed off from Johor in 1609. As head of the Dutch factory at Batu Sawar, Obelaer had the unpleasant task of briefing the royal court on the recent conclusion of a truce between the Dutch Republic and the Spanish and Portuguese empires. In the following year, he is reported to have stood by help-lessly when Raja Bongsu and his pro-Dutch faction at the court were pushed aside in favor of a formal peace with the Portuguese in October 1610.[82]

---

81   CMJ, 350; and below, p. 157.

82   SMS, 110-11.

Just who was this Jacques Obelaer? Evidence preserved in the Torre do Tombo Archives in Lisbon suggests that he later defected to the Portuguese and may have been spying for them in Batu Sawar while he was serving at the VOC factory there. There is one specific document preserved in Lisbon that we should be interested in: it survives in the *Collecção de São Vicente* (Collection St. Vincent), was written in Goa, and dated 4 April, 1612.[83] Here it is intimated that Jacques Obelaer had been born in Bruges in the Spanish Netherlands. He had served as the Dutch factor at Johor and, being Catholic, had defected to the Portuguese side. His flight from Johor first brought him to Melaka and later to Goa where he gave the authorities a testimony. What did Obelaer tell the Portuguese? He claimed that the Dutch were so disillusioned by not being able to pluck Melaka from the Portuguese that they were now hoping to "erect a fortress on an island that divides the Straits and where the vessels heading off to China pass through".[84] This location, Obelaer further underscored, was at a distance of about 5 *legoas*— or about 31 kilometers—from "the Johor kingdom". If this distance was estimated as the crow flies, then the "Johor" in question here was most probably around Johor Lama and not the royal capital Batu Sawar.

As company factor in Johor, Obelaer would have been privy to plans the VOC was hatching at its base in Banten at the time. If Matelieff, and Verhoeff after him, had been vague about the exact location of any new Dutch fortification around the Johor River estuary and the Straits, the men-on-the-spot evidently had much clearer ideas. Obelaer's testimony is unambiguous about the intended location: an island that separates two Straits about 30-odd kilometers from Johor Lama. Now where might that be? It is present-day Sentosa.

---

83 ANTT, *Colecção de São Vicente*, livro 26, fol. 130 recto.
84 Ibid.

Prior to the opening up of the so-called Governor's Strait after 1616,[85] there were two known Straits of Singapore: the Old and the New Straits. The Old Strait passed along the northern shore of Sentosa, the New Strait by contrast passed along its southwestern shore.[86] The dividing point of the two Straits is the northwestern tip where the remains of Fort Siloso (built by the British) stand. It is uncanny that the Dutch were thinking about constructing a fort at the very same location where Jacques de Coutre proposed one around the same time—but De Coutre submitted his plan to the king of Spain and Portugal.[87] His detailed description of the location and the surroundings of his proposed fortification have been published in my earlier book *Jacques de Coutre's Singapore and Johor (c.1594-1625)* and can be recommended as further reading here. De Coutre—like Obelaer—explains why this particular location is so strategically important: this is "where the vessels heading off to China pass through".[88] If one controls this single nodal point, one effectively gains a stranglehold of the maritime arteries connecting ports in India with ports around the South China Sea. Where Obelaer and De Coutre differ is in the purpose of their respective forts: for De Coutre, supporting the Iberian side, the proposed fortification on Sentosa was to control Dutch privateering activity in and around the Singapore Straits. This was one of the favorite hotspots for the Dutch to attack and capture fully-laden Portuguese vessels from China on their way to Melaka and Goa as they

---

85   See SMS, 150-1; and Borschberg, "The Straits of Singapore: Continuity, Change and Confusion," in *Sketching the Straits. A Compilation of the Lecture Series on the Charles Dyce Collection*, ed. Irene Lim (Singapore: NUS Museums, 2004), 33-47.

86   See the list of place names (*New Strait; Old Strait of Singapore*).

87   JCSJ, 17-27, 76-8; JDC, 227-41.

88   ANTT, *Colecção de São Vicente*, livro 26, fol. 130 recto.

did with the *Santa Catarina* in 1603.[89] For the Dutch, as reported by Obelaer, the intended purpose of this fort was to squeeze off traffic heading to Melaka and Portuguese ports around the Bay of Bengal and beyond. The similarity of the two projects is quite striking— and raises an additional question: as the two plans are so similar, might there be a connection between them? As a rule, historians should refrain from engaging in speculation. Their task is to develop arguments that are supported by evidence. What historians can do is put questions and issues on the table for further research and discussion, and this is precisely what I want to do here: is it possible that De Coutre and Obelaer might have met at one time? Let's look at the evidence at hand: both are from the city of Bruges in the Spanish Netherlands, both had spent time on the Malay Peninsula and had been to Johor on business or had lived there; and both were in Goa in the year 1612. Are these just sheer coincidences? How many citizens of Bruges might there have been staying in Goa at the beginning of the 17th century? Might Obelaer not have looked up or met Jacques de Coutre and his brother Joseph? If so, would it not be likely that they discussed what the Dutch were getting up to in a region they were both intimately familiar with? I have more than just a hunch that there is likely to be a connection between the two Jacques—De Coutre and Obelaer—but I do not have the evidence yet to conclusively prove it.

89   See SMS, 71-5, 92-7; also P. Borschberg, "The Seizure of the Santa Catarina off Singapore: Dutch Freebooting, the Portuguese Empire and Intra-Asian Trade at the Dawn of the Seventeenth Century," *Revista de Cultura*, International Edition, 11 (2004): 11–25; Borschberg, "The Seizure of the Sta. Catarina Revisited: The Portuguese Empire in Asia, VOC Politics and the Origins of the Dutch-Johor Alliance (c. 1602–1616)," *JSEAS*, 33.1 (2002): 31–62; also Borschberg, "Portuguese, Spanish and Dutch plans to construct a Fort in the Straits of Singapore, ca. 1584-1625," *Archipel*, 63.2 (2003): 55-88.

Singapore's near miss

The preceding section covering Dutch plans to construct a fort on Sentosa is evidence that Admiral Matelieff—
and the early European colonial powers at large—had
Singapore on their proverbial radar screen. This insight will
be strengthened in the present section with reference to
Matelieff's plans for finding a permanent base for the VOC
in Asia.

As has been stated earlier, one of the principal moti-
vations for penning his memorials was a deep sense of dis-
satisfaction over the way the VOC was conducting business
and diplomacy across the region. There were several recurring issues raised in the course of most of the memorials.
One we have already mentioned: the need to abolish the fleet
commander system and instead appoint a governor-general
with plenipotentiary power within the territories covered
by the Company's charter east of the Cape of Good Hope.[90]
Arguably, the most important recurring theme is the urgency
of establishing what Matelieff called a rendezvous. What the
admiral had in mind here is a centrally-located base in Asia.

When Matelieff faulted the early VOC system of
appointing fleet commanders, he was not just thinking about
creating greater consistency in dealing with the Company's
Asian allies, he was also hoping to improve operational efficiency and preparedness for war. Now, if the appointment
of a governor-general (supported in his deliberations by a
council)[91] was to bring stability and consistency in imple-
menting company policies across the Asian region, the
establishment of a rendezvous was to offer administrative
support and act as a central logistics node. Early fleet com-

---

90   CMJ, 133-4.

91   A committee formed in 1609 to advise the governor-general of
      the VOC. The committee was composed of both ordinary (or
      standing) and extra-ordinary members. See CMJ, 506.

Right: The city of Palembang (artist unknown). The Hague: National Archives of the Netherlands, 4.VEL 1138.

manders sometimes found it difficult to find sufficient cargo for their homebound voyage, and the spice market was organized in such a way that a given clove or nutmeg harvest had already been committed or sold while it was still hanging on the bush or tree. Waiting for a new harvest to ripen or bringing in supplies from elsewhere was a time-consuming affair: ships' officers and mates still had to be paid their monthly wages, whether or not they were actually doing anything.[92]

Matelieff's solution was to create a centrally-located, permanent base in the East Indies where goods and commodities could be brought in gradually from factories dotted around India, East and Southeast Asia. Here, ships belonging to the blue-water fleet from Europe could quickly discharge their cargo, reload, and swiftly set sail again on the homebound voyage. As a means of accelerating turn-around time and also in having sufficient naval firepower at the disposal of the Company, he suggested establishing a merchant fleet that would be separate from the blue-water fleet from Europe. This merchant fleet would be stationed in Asia to serve only the needs of intra-Asian trade.[93] Matelieff's basic reasoning about the rendezvous was this:[94]

"First of all, we must choose a rendezvous or meeting place in the Indies, where all ships from these lands[95] can easily call and take in fresh supplies. All provisions, foodstuffs and ammunition of war

---

92   CMJ, 287.

93   Gaastra, *The Dutch East India Company*, 39-40, "As well as this [Matelieff] saw the possibility, later to be so fiercely argued by [Jan Pieterszoon] Coen, that the VOC could fend for itself in Asia by setting up and intra-Asian trading network."

94   CMJ, 255.

95   Read: from the Dutch Republic.

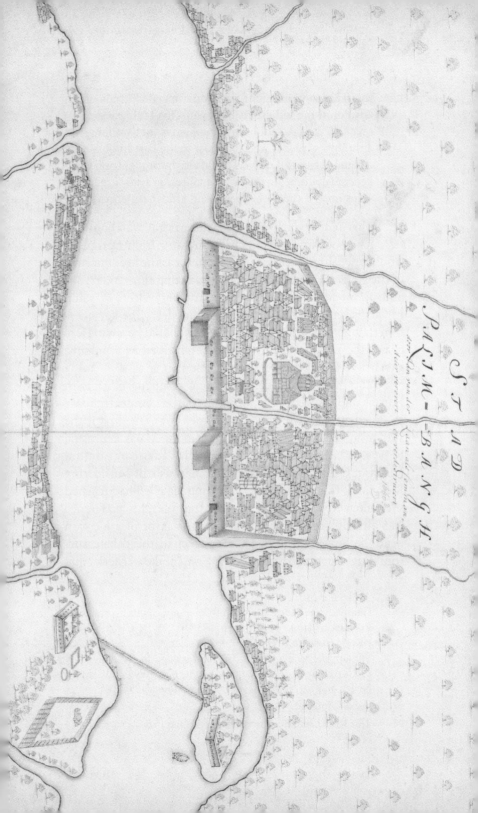

STAD
PALIM-BANG H

100 On van der
200 On dit conflian
aliax verviert
en verdeurt

should also be brought there and amassed gradually, for in the Indies it is impossible to obtain these quickly. This has not been attempted at all thus far, although it is what we need most in the East Indies. All goods from all regions could also be brought and kept safely there, for regional navigation with large ships involves a lot of expenses and inconvenience."

This rendezvous would be the central warehouse in Asia for goods and equipment brought in from Europe. It would offer support services and also act as the headquarters of the governor-general. In conceptualizing this rendezvous and its broader functions, the Portuguese viceroy's setup in Goa is known to have served as a model.[96] The key question though was where the rendezvous should be sited. Here again, the region around Singapore emerged as a possible site, before finally yielding to a location on Java.

The decade-long debate among company officials in Europe and Asia over the founding of the new central base assumed at least two important dimensions. The first is the shift away of the VOC's attention from the Malay Peninsula to Java. When Matelieff was penning his advice to Admiral Paul van Caerden in January 1608, he was still considering Melaka for this purpose.[97] By the time Matelieff had reached the Dutch Republic in September that year, his preference was already beginning to crystallize in favor of a location near the Sunda Strait.[98] Another facet in the debate surrounding the rendezvous focused on the key criteria that

---

96 Gaastra, *The Dutch East India Company*, 39-40; Cornelis G. Roelofsen, "Hugo de Groot en de VOC", in *De Hollandse jaren van Hugo de Groot (1582-1621). Lezingen van het colloquium ter gelegenheid van de 350-ste sterfdag van Hugo de Groot ('s-Gravenhage: 31 augustus - 1 september 1995)*, ed. H.J.M. Nellen and J. Trapman (Hilversum: Verloren, 1996), 57.

97 See document 3.

98 This strait separates the islands of Sumatra and Java.

this location would need to meet, the most important being that, if possible, it should be accessible all year round. Time, after all, is money.

In his memorials, the admiral considered six possible sites for the rendezvous. They are, from north to south: Aceh, Melaka, Singapore and the Johor River estuary, Palembang,[99] Banten and Jeyakerta. Other locations had been mentioned by other VOC agents as a potential site, including Pulau Condor[100] or a location on the Malukus or Bandas. But on closer investigation, these were not deemed to represent sufficiently central locations. The merits of each of these were discussed in varying depth and detail. Each was duly weighed for its ease of access, position within the regional trading networks, as well as for its broader geo-strategic location. There are, however, additional facets in the admiral's deliberations that are well worth exploring in greater depth.

The first concerns the region surrounding the Singapore Straits and the Johor River estuary. In 1605-6, the VOC's preference was to take Melaka from the Portuguese and use this as their base. When this was the goal, attention remained broadly fixed on the peninsula. Subsequently, after failing to pluck Melaka from the Portuguese, attention moved southwards toward the Singapore Straits region and the Johor River estuary. The Singapore Straits were acknowledged as an important maritime artery which rendered the islands and the surrounding lands strategic locations. The Dutch had already recognized this in 1603 when Jacob van Heemskerck attacked and plundered the Portuguese carrack *Santa Catarina* off the eastern coast of Singapore. For

---

99   Port and polity located in central-eastern Sumatra. Though chiefly famous in the context of the pepper trade, Palembang was also a center for eaglewood, beeswax, and lakawood. See JDC, 374.

100   See the list of place names (*Pulau Condor*).

45

decades thereafter, the Singapore Straits served as a hunting ground for VOC naval patrols that scoured the waters between Karimun and Pedra Branca[101] in search of easy Iberian prey.[102] As discussed in the previous section, the Dutch must have recognized and acknowledged the strategic location of Singapore if they were planning to construct a fortress on an island that separated the two straits. Through these all ships heading for ports around the South China Sea and the western Pacific had to pass.

Despite these evident geo-strategic and locational advantages, a number of factors increasingly came to count against the Singapore-Johor nexus as a potential site for the future VOC rendezvous: in the age of sail, it was not easily accessible all year round—ships had to wait for the shift of the monsoon winds for several months. Then there was the lack of food supplies from the hinterland: Matelieff quickly realized that Portuguese Melaka needed to import almost all of its food from outside, and that seriously exposed it to one of the worst perils of siege warfare: starvation. He had observed very similar conditions at Batu Sawar, highlighting that the local population did not engage much in farming.[103] A location around the Singapore Straits and the Johor River estuary was therefore unlikely to be any different. Added to this was the unwillingness of the Johor rulers to permit the Dutch to construct a fort or let their two peoples live in close proximity to one another.

At the time of drafting the commission and standing orders for the first VOC Governor-General Pieter Both in the final weeks of 1609, the VOC directors in Europe were still contemplating the Singapore Straits-Johor River nexus as a potential site for their future base in Asia.[104] By that date

---

101 Rock formation at the eastern entrance of the Singapore Strait.
102 See SMS, 157-83.
103 CMJ, 192, and below p. 109.
104 Transcripts of the governor-general's first commission are

however, Matelieff had already moved his attention away from the Malay Peninsula and set his sights on an entirely different location altogether: western Java. In late August 1610, the admiral explained to Grotius that the region around the Johor River estuary was actually not a very suitable location after all:[105]

> "It has come to my attention, however, that the Gentlemen Directors in their latest instruction to Governor-[General] Pieter Both have indicated the Hook of Johor[106] to him as the place to keep his residence (as a consequence, that would become our rendezvous). I then did not think it necessary to write to you against it, since it was sufficiently rebutted in my previous writings,[107] before that instruction had been written. Moreover, the Gentlemen Directors have been informed with the latest arriving ships that the king of Johor is completely opposed to creating a fortress in his country, so that need will make us understand what we cannot understand by reason.

found in P.J.A.N. van Rietbergen, *De Eerste Landvoogd Pieter Both (1568-1615): Gouverneur-Generaal van Nederlandsch-Indië*, 2 vols. (Zutphen: Walberg Pers, 1987), as well as in J.A. van der Chijs, ed., *Nederlandsch-Indisch Plakaat-boek, 1602-1811*, 17 vols. (Batavia: Landsdrukkerij, and The Hague: Martinus Nijhoff, 1885-1900). The relevant instruction is found in art. 11, (Van der Chijs, *Nederlandsch-Indisch Placcaatboek*, I, 8): Governor-General Both was instructed to deliberate "… at which location you want to establish yourself for the time being, be it on Banten, Johor or elsewhere." (Translated from the original Dutch). See also BOC, II.1, 339n4.

105   CMJ, 346.

106   Also known as the Hook of Berbukit from period cartographic materials, the Hook of Johor corresponds roughly to present-day Tanjung Pengerang which is located across the Johor River estuary from Changi Point.

107   Read: memorials.

Printed etching of the Portuguese-held town of Melaka in 1606. Taken from Isaac Commelin's printed collection of early Dutch travelogues published in Amsterdam in 1646 in 2 volumes. This illustration is taken from vol. 2, "Vande treffelijcke Reyse, gedaen naer de Oost-Indien ende China ... door ... Cornelis Matelief de Ionge" (Historic Narrative of the Excellent Voyage made to the East Indies and China by Cornelis Matelieff de Jonge), between fols. 28 and 29. (Leiden University Library, special collections, 348 C 10).

In this context, the following citation merits repetition:[108]

> ... [T]he rendezvous at Johor is unsuitable, because one cannot reach it at every time of the year. It is also unsuitable to navigate and sail to all locations, and then there is the jealousy of the aforementioned

---

108   CMJ, 348.

king [of Johor] who does not want to concede us a
fortress there, as I and Pieter Willemsz. [Verhoeff]
after me have found out by experience."

This document of 31 August, 1610, is very significant
for the history of Singapore in two respects: first, it shows
that the geo-strategic and locational significance of the
Singapore Straits and its surrounding lands and islands
were well recognized and acknowledged by leading officers
of the VOC almost right from their arrival in the Straits
region. They seriously contemplated the locational merits
of the Singapore-Johor nexus, but after careful deliberation,
decided against establishing their Asian base in this region.
Second, the decision not to establish the rendezvous in the
Singapore-Johor River estuary region marked a permanent
shift of attention away from the Malay Peninsula and its surrounding islands altogether. The VOC would hereafter focus
on the Sunda Strait and northwestern Java. Here, Matelieff
and the VOC directors weighed three possible locations for
the future rendezvous: Banten, Jeyakerta, or a then sparsely
populated estuary of the Tanjung Burung River located to
the west of Jeyakerta. With reference to the former, Matelieff
underscored:[109]

> "The city of Banten, albeit well-situated, is not
> only very unwholesome, but also has a very young
> king[110]—fourteen or fifteen years old—who is
> impossible to negotiate with; moreover, his coun-
> cil is so divided by factionalism that one cannot
> accomplish anything."

For these essentially political reasons, the admiral's

---

109   CMJ, 255-6.
110   A reference to the adolescent Pangeran Ratu who, after 1638,
      ruled Banten as Abulmafakhir Mahmud Abdul Qadir. See also
      CMJ, 80, 501, 532.

Left: Full portrait of Laurens Reael by C. van der Voort, c.1620. Rijksmuseum Amsterdam, SK-A-3741.

choice thus fell on the latter two locations:[111]

> "My best advice would be, therefore, that we negoti-
> ate with the king of Jeyakerta,[112] so that we can build
> a fortress either in his city or at the aforementioned
> freshwater river;[113] the Sunda Strait can be sailed
> in every season, either to Banten or to Jeyakerta, if
> one has rounded the Cape of Good Hope and one
> doesn't have to endure the monsoon."

Admittedly, Matelieff was not alone in putting to paper such deliberations about the benefits of a location near the Sunda Strait. In their instructions to the first Governor-General Pieter Both, the VOC directors thought it "very advisable to enter into closer communication and alliance with the king of Jeyakerta, to wit: to desire of him a suitable place to build a fort there" which would "serve to Our satisfaction as a rendezvous for the whole of the Indian nav-

---

111 CMJ, 256.

112 This ruler is variously named in other sources as Pangerang Jayawikarta or Wijayakama. The comment by Hoesein Djaja-diningrat in his doctoral thesis *Critische beschouwing van de Sadjarah Bantĕn: Bijdrage ter kenschetsing van de Javaansche geschiedschrijving* (Haarlem: Joh. Enschedé en Zonen, 1913), 167, is noteworthy, where he explains that the name of the "Pangeran van Djakĕtra" mentioned in the *Sajarah Bantĕn* (Kawis Adimarta) differs from what we read in the Dutch sources, where he is referred to as Widjajakrama. In a footnote featured on that same page, Djajadiningrat also refers to the name 'Pn. [i.e. Pangeran] Djajawikarta'. He thinks this name, Jayawikarta, to represent a variant of the title 'Pangeran of Jay-akarta'." I would like to thank my former colleague Prof. M.C. Ricklefs for resolving the identity of this ruler.

113 Read: Tanjung Burung River.

igation and of Our ships...."[114] In a report to the directors written a few years later and dated 18 July 1616, Governor-General Laurens Reael—the third VOC governor-general—concurred that the Sunda Strait was the best possible location for the rendezvous and easily also the most comfortable site in all of East Indies. Since the rulers of Banten and Jeyakerta also controlled both sides of the Sunda Strait, he thought it of great importance to work toward building and maintaining a sound working relationship with them. In a letter penned a year later, 17 December 1617, Reael conceded:[115]

> "In our opinion the location Johor will not serve well as a rendezvous, even less that we should engage our means with [its] impoverished king, and the same we also feel about Ceylon."

As a location for the rendezvous, Johor was not completely off the table and remained a matter of internal Company debate for some years to come. While some leading members of the VOC and government were edging away from Johor as a potential location, other Company officials were still willing to seriously contemplate it. One can cite in this context, for example, the letter of Peter Seeger to the Gentlemen Directors dated 5 December 1612, in which he continues to list Johor with Pulau Condor as a realistic and viable choice.[116]

> "Concerning the coasts of Johor or the city of Banten on Java, at one of these places we have to also found a rendezvous, with a good contingent of soldiers, to

---

114 Van der Chijs, *Nederlandsch-Indisch Placaatboek*, I, 14, article 23 of Both's instructions.

115 W.Ph. Coolhaas, ed., *Generale Missiven van Gouverneurs' Generaal en Raden aan Heren XVII der Verenigde Oostindische Compagnie, part I, 1610-1638* (The Hague : Martinus Nijhoff, 1960), 79.

116 JO, IV, 6, 7.

safeguard and defend the trade from China and the coast. Otherwise one will be subject to fire and bellicose action …. I say, venerable Gentlemen, issue an order to establish a rendezvous, be it on Pulau Condor or Johor or elsewhere, which one here shall find the best and most convenient."

By December 1613, a decision on the rendezvous had still not been taken, and in his private letter to Grotius dated 13 December, Matelieff expressed his concerns about the delay: [117]

"The matter of creating a rendezvous is the most necessary of all that one could think of, in order to survey all the difficulties in the Indies from there, as if from a high tower; and to be so powerful there that we would have a prompt remedy for all kinds of occurrences. …

The longer the Gentlemen [directors] delay doing this, the worse it is for our state. For of this we can be sure: things will come to a bad ending for us at Banten someday, for the barbarians do not respect us and we do not have the power to command respect. Nobody tries to establish security for our state, since they are only servants on three-year contracts without reward or punishment—and when they come home, they dare not speak up, fearing the Directors' displeasure."

For Matelieff, the dithering and indecision had simply lasted for too long. But how warranted are his carpings really about the Gentlemen Directors and their alleged procrastination in finding a location for the rendezvous? According to the VOC advocate and historian Pieter van Dam, who wrote at the turn of the 17th and 18th centuries, the Gentlemen

---

117   CMJ, 367-7.

Directors had decided around mid-November 1611 to set up a committee comprising one delegate from each of the six chambers and charged with ascertaining the best location for the rendezvous.[118] Most unfortunately, however, no materials, recommendations or decisions appear to survive of this secret committee. But the manuscript bundles VOC 99-100, preserved in the National Archives of the Netherlands in The Hague, do contain the minutes of the meetings held by the Gentlemen Seventeen in this time period. These minutes are meticulously compiled treasure-troves that contain valuable information, right down to the seating arrangements during each of the meetings. Here we also find further particulars regarding the Director's deliberations on the rendezvous. This is not the time and occasion to delve into the finer details raised and discussed during the meetings, but I think it is of some value to ascertain what options were on the table and, how they were whittled down, and when a given option was eventually dropped.

A careful reading of these minutes reveals that the Directors, over several meetings, weighed the various potential locations for the rendezvous from 1608 onwards, in other words, after Matelieff's return from Asia. By the meeting of March 1614—just a few months after Matelieff's letter to Grotius expressing the urgent need to select a rendezvous cited above—the Directors had finally whittled down their choice to a site in the vicinity of the Sunda Strait. From this point onward, locations around the Melaka and Singapore Straits, Aceh and Palembang as well as all other locations—Pulau Condor, the Bandas and the Malukus—were no longer being considered. Hereafter, however, the decision-making process appears to have ground to a halt at least until late 1617.[119] As Frederik de Haan commented

---

118   BOC, I.1, 214.

119   The Hague, National Archives of the Netherlands (1.04.02), VOC no. 100, resolution of 15-16 August, 1612, 183-4; resolu-

Portrait of Jan Pietersz. Coen, copy, (artist unknown), late 18th century. Rijksmusem Amsterdam, M-SK-A-4528-00.

tion March 1614, 234, where under the heading "concerning the choice of a rendezvous" the locations Jacatra, Banten, and the Straits of Sunda generally are mentioned as the preferred locations. Similar resolutions follow in the sessions of 9-20 September, 1614, ibid., 264; 14 August 1617, ibid., 388; and 28 October to 4 November 1617, 413, 428, 437. Translated from the original Dutch.

in his work *Oud Batavia—Gedenkboek* (Old Batavia—Commemorative Volume), no decision had been reached on the location of the rendezvous when troops were ready to storm the walls of Jeyakerta.[120] By this date, developments in Jeyakerta were unfolding in such a way that Governor-General Jan Pieterszoon Coen, who had also clamored for the founding of the rendezvous for many years,[121] would present the Directors in Europe with a *fait accompli*.[122] Although Jeyakerta had been one of the possible locations for some time, problems on the ground involving the VOC, the English East India Company and Banten coalesced into military action that triggered the fall of Jeyakerta on 30 May, 1619.[123] The name for the new rendezvous had already

---

120   F. de Haan, *Oud Batavia; Gedenkboek uitgegeven door het Bataviaasch Genootschap van Kunsten en Wetenschappen naar aanleiding van het driehonderdjarig bestaan der stad in 1919*, 3 vols. (Batavia: Kolff, 1922-3), I, 10.

121   CMJ, 364, "This Coen is clamoring loudly for a rendezvous. ... Your Honor [i.e Grotius] should read the letter and give it to the Lord Advocate [Oldenbarnevelt] as well; it is dat. November 10, 1614, from Banten, by the same Coen." Coen's letter of 10 November, 1614 has been transcribed and published in full length in H.T. Colenbrander and W.Ph. Coolhaas, ed., *Jan Pieterszoon Coen: Bescheiden Omtrent Zijn Bedrijf in Indië*, 9 vols. (The Hague: Martinus Nijhoff, 1919-53), I, 52-92; and partially reproduced in JO, IV, 20-4. Translated from the original Dutch.

122   According to the last report filed by Governor-General Both dated 10 November, 1614, Coen had arrived at the Banten factory earlier that year. He left a deep impression on the governor-general who judged him "a person well experienced in trade and in matters of state, very honest and modest in his lifestyle, always hard working without wasting any time." (Translated from Dutch). Coen received notification of his appointment to governor-general June 1618. See also De Haan, *Oud Batavia. Gedenkboek*, I, 19

123   The fall of Jeyakerta was also taken to be the day of Dutch Batavia's founding. See De Haan, *Oud Batavia. Gedenkboek*, I, 38.

been chosen some time earlier. On 31 October, 1617, the Gentlemen Directors wrote to the governor-general that the rendezvous, when finally chosen, be named Batavia.[124]

The shift of attention southward marked a crucial transition with long-term historical repercussions: the Malay Peninsula would no longer stand at the forefront of attention, and the VOC's focus would hereafter be placed on Java, and to an extent, also on the spice-yielding islands of the Malukus and the Bandas. In 1641, Melaka was finally snatched from the Portuguese after a protracted military campaign,[125] but it would now have to yield to the primacy of the VOC's Asian base Batavia—the new name of Jeyakerta under Dutch rule.

Batu Sawar and Kota Seberang

The previous sections have addressed the geo-strategic location of the Singapore-Johor River nexus. Let us move our attention upstream to the former Johor royal residence of Batu Sawar. Nearby, slightly downstream, was its smaller sister settlement on the opposite river bank named Kota Seberang. From the *Journal* as well as from Matelieff's memorials, we can collate a number of important statements that help us visualize what Batu Sawar—and Johor at large—was like at the dawn of the 17th century. The single most important statement is without doubt, a brief description of the two settlements which was penned following the admiral's visit to the Batu Sawar court in 1606:

> "The town of Batu Sawar is situated up the Johor River, approximately five or six [Dutch nautical] miles from the sea.[126] The river [there] is very beau-

---

124   Ibid., I, 10.

125   SMS, 183-7.

126   That is about 37-44 kilometers from the sea.

Right: Pepper grows on a vine that supports itself on other plants or on man-made stands. This picture was taken in Sumatra around 2002. Peter Borschberg, private collection.

tiful, wide and deep,[127] [and depending on the tide] flows either up or down along the banks before the city,[128] but here the water is fresh. The land is mostly flat. The population generally lives along the river. The houses stand on stilts. What is meant by the term 'fortress' consists of two things: one is Batu Sawar and the other situated on the opposite bank of the river is called Kota Seberang. Batu Sawar measures about 1,300 *treden* in circumference,[129] is square in its layout, and feature high palisades that are closely lined up against one another and measure 40 feet high.[130] There are some fortifications which cover the flank,[131] but these are not well constructed. It is situated on a level plain close by the river. The closest hills are situated about a quarter

---

127 RWME, 483, where the depth of the water is given at 5-5.5 meters and the width of the river at about 90 meters.

128 This observation implies that the waters of the Johor River at Batu Sawar are influenced by changes in the oceanic tides, but the location was too far removed from the sea for salt water to enter the Johor River with the tide. See also RWME, 483. My own observations at the archaeological site at Batu Sawar confirm this description.

129 Lit. "steps"; a Dutch unit to measure distance, here about 975 meters.

130 Here about 11 meters high.

131 Reference is here most probably to smaller auxiliary fortifications which cover the flank of another fortification structure, similar to the ones found at the archaeological site in Johor Lama. These would have covered blind spots at Kota Seberang. A visit to the archaeological site confirms that there is indeed a bend in the river slightly downstream that creates such a blind spot. See also RWME, 438-9.

of a mile[132] from there. It is easily possible to divert
the river around the city. Inside, the city is densely
populated featuring straw houses, except for the
residence of the king and of some other noblemen,
which are constructed of wood. There are an estimated three to four thousand fighting men in Batu
Sawar and Kota Seberang together, but most of the
population lives outside the walled city. In times of

---

132   About a kilometer.

danger, these people completely burn down their homes and head into the walled city, because they are able to quickly rebuild a house, each man with his slaves. ... Kota Seberang may measure about 400 or 500 *treden*[133] in circumference and is also square in its layout. Not many people live here, and where they live there are also [wooden] palisades along the river bank. The land is flat, and is flooded during all spring tides..."[134]

The description found in the *Journal* stands out for the detail which it provides to the reader. It contrasts, say, with the travelogue of Verhoeff which covers the admiral's visit to Batu Sawar in January and February 1609, but contains no description of the city or its location. A close reading of the *Journal* and the memorials reveals why Matelieff was interested, and what he specifically took an interest in: the geographic setting of the town and its security installations. At the time of his visit, the admiral had a good look around the settlements of Batu Sawar and Kota Seberang and had suggested improvements for beefing up their security and protection against future Portuguese attacks. He feared that when Johor was not protected by the presence of a Dutch fleet, Melaka would launch a raid on Batu Sawar and the other upstream towns. Matelieff was right: the Portuguese spent much of 1608 blockading the Johor River and launching sporadic attacks.[135] The admiral underscored in his

---

133 About 300-375 meters.

134 A copy of this Dutch-language description of Batu Sawar and Kota Seberang with commentary is also found in RWME, 482-3; for another English translation see GPFT, appendix 11, 208-9.

135 It is known from a certificate of services issued to one Nicolau de Soveral, for 20 July 1608, that he had participated in a campaign against Johor that comprised five galleys and seven ships. These had arrived in the Singapore Straits and also attacked vessels anchored in the port of Johor. See Lisbon, Na-

memorial of 12 November, 1608: [136]

> "... [W]e ought to try fortifying the city first; this
> would not work without using some harsh words,
> or else in such a way as would be best put into prac-
> tice, not discussed in writing. The young king, Raja
> Seberang, would be favorably inclined to this; the
> old one [Ala'udin] is more capable of drinking than
> of ruling. It would cost us 4,000 or 5,000 reals,[137]
> but if we made the investment we could collect it
> in due course; or if that went badly, we would still
> set back the enemy with it to such a degree that it
> would be of much greater importance to us. We
> should see if the situation is still as it was when I
> was there. Keeping a big garrison there would bring
> high costs with it; but after fortifying the city, the
> Malays would be somewhat reassured. Once the
> city had been reconstructed, we could reassure the
> Malays with 50 or 60 white soldiers, so that they
> would stay together and be all right; unless there
> came an army larger than I imagine can be called
> up from the Indies."

In order to improve protection of the towns, he suggested some improvements to their defenses. The texts,
however, tell us that his suggestions met either with little
interest or outright resistance. Perhaps this was just another
one of those rifts he had to address and deal with: the strategy of the locals was to burn down their own settlement
when the enemy advanced and then flee into the jungle, or
at least move deeper inland. Matelieff maintained that this

---

tional Library of Portugal, *Viscondes da Lapa*, Caixa 3, "Maço
4, no. 1", fol. 6 verso-7 recto. The exact dates for this campaign,
however, are not established.

136   CMJ, 271.

137   Read: reals-of-eight; about 108.5-135.5 kilograms of coin-
grade silver.

Right: Rare commodities traded by the Europeans in the early modern period. From top to bottom: sandalwood chips in West Timor; camphor resin oozing from the bark of a camphor tree in Sarawak, Malaysia; close-up of a porcupine bezoar in Miri, Sarawak. Peter Borschberg, private collection.

was not an option for the Dutch because they had assets and infrastructure that needed protection. In Batu Sawar, that included most significantly, their factory full of trading goods.

The Dutch had established their factory at the time of Jacob van Heemskerck's visit to Batu Sawar and the seizure of the *Santa Catarina* in 1603. As is explained in a letter by Heemskerck to his directors dated 27 August 1603, the first supervisor was Jacob Buys (sometimes Buyzen) who had needed lots of persuasion to assume the role of head of operations at Batu Sawar. At the time of Matelieff's visit in 1606, Buys was relieved and the admiral's former personal secretary, Abraham van den Broeck, was installed as his successor. The newly-appointed VOC supervisor would serve in Johor for about two and a half years between September 1606 and March 1609.

Batu Sawar marketplace for pepper

Johor had a center of trade that had steadily grown during the second half of the 16th century. There are several testimonies, mainly from the Portuguese side, that attest to the brisk business being conducted here. Jacques de Coutre, who had visited Batu Sawar on several occasions during the 1590s and early 1600s, described it as a place where there were many merchants who "lived only from merchandise and from sailing from one country to another".[138] Similar observations were made in the brief of Stalpaert van der

---

138   CDJ, 241; JCSJ, 29, 88.

Wiele, dating from around this period. Here it is reported that Johor is a "famous trading city" where a "lot of pepper" could be obtained.[139] The same point is echoed in the letter by Van Heemskerk to his directors dated 27 August, 1603. In this, he claimed that Johor was "clearly the most suitable place in all of the East Indies to load pepper and sell textiles from Cambay[140] and S[ão] Thomé".[141]

The VOC historian Pieter van Dam, writing at the turn of the 17th and 18th centuries, extolled the significance of Batu Sawar, though he admitted that the land of the Johor mainland itself yielded little: [142]

> "From the beginning the [Dutch] Company main-
> tained a factory in Johor, [a kingdom] which bor-
> ders the land of Melaka; not that [Johor] is a land
> that has, or can deliver, much of itself, but in that
> it is well located for trade, and it always had a lot of
> maritime traffic."

Not surprising then, Batu Sawar's status as a market for pepper was also known to Matelieff. In his memorial of June 1607, he briefly laid out the different main branches of intra-Asian trade. With reference to pepper, he noted under point 1: "Pepper to be obtained at Banten, Johor, Patani, Kedah[143]

---

139   JCSJ, 32.

140   Port and city of the Gujarat Sultanate and a major trading city. It was renowned for a number of goods such as cotton textiles. See JDC, 355.

141   H. Grotius, *Jure Praedae Commentarius: Commentary on the Law of Prize and Booty*, ed. M.J. van Ittersum (Indianapolis: Liberty Fund, 2006), appendix II, document 4, 539.

142   BOC, II.1, 328; CSCJ, 34.

143   River, port, settlement and polity in the northwestern regions on the Malay Peninsula important in the context of the pepper and tin trade. In the 16th and 17th centuries, the Portuguese regarded Kedah as a vassal or client state of Siam. It was attacked and overrun by Aceh in 1619.

and Aceh."[144]

Realistically, how much pepper are we looking at? Very few of the records of the VOC factory at Batu Sawar survive and these relate mainly to the period around 1608—in other words during the time when Van den Broeck was head of operations there.

In his report titled "Expenses and Provisions for the Fleet done at Johor" covering Dutch cargo loadings for the period January-July 1608, several consignments of pepper are recorded.

The first consisted of 46,573 *kati*[145] (about 27,944 kilograms) with an assigned book value of about 5,474 guilders (58.24 kilograms of silver) and a second comprising 76,819 *kati* (about 46,091 kilograms) worth about 9,751 guilders (about 103.37 kilograms of silver) are recorded.

Among the other items traded were printed and plain Indian cotton textiles as well as unminted gold, aloes or eaglewood,[146] kalambak,[147] resins like camphor[148] and

---

144   CMJ, 337, and below, p. 123.

145   An East and Southeast Asian unit to measure weight; each about 600 grams. See JDC, 326.

146   A type of odoriferous aloeswood drenched in its own resin that, when burned, releases a sweet, pleasant odor. Erédia describes it as "a tall stout tree with leaves like an olive: the pitch inside is bitter and oily." See JDC, 318; MGED, 26; SMS, 337.

147   Highest-grade aloeswood, usually from Champa or the Malay Peninsula and Sumatra widely used in early modern Europe and Asia as medicine as well as in the production of incense. Erédia claims it was "derived from the oiliest pith of the [aloeswood] tree." See JDC, 325–6; MGED, 26; SMS, 337.

148   See the glossary (*camphor*).

benzoin,[149] turtle [shells],[150] beeswax,[151] bezoars[152] and rough diamonds.

In his memorial "Discourse on the Possibilities of Trade for the VOC in the East Indies" dated 12 November, 1608, Matelieff continued to acknowledge Batu Sawar as one of the principal pepper suppliers to the Company, but expressed concern about Johor's political scene. In proposing a reorganization of the way the VOC conducted its business in the East, the admiral reasoned:[153]

"I think that over time the Indians could also bring as much pepper to our community there as the Company would need. But for now, one should still keep a clerk and two assistants at Johor, until one would see where the Johor cause was going. So I conclude that as far as pepper is concerned, Jeyakerta and Banten with the addition of Johor should bring us enough pepper for the time being, without our having to keep a factory at Aceh and Patani for that purpose; for it would certainly be brought to us at Jeyakerta and Johor...."

By contrast, Matelieff found it impossible to say any-

---

149   A tree resin used in medicine as well as in the production of incense. According to Erédia, it derives from a "tall stout tree. The gum or liquor which oozes and exudes from the clefts and holes in the bark" is called benzoin. See JDC, 306; MGED, 26; SMS, 337.

150   *Karet*, as turtle shell is known in Malay, was used for making certain personal luxury instruments (such as combs) or ornaments.

151   Beeswax was widely used for making candles as well as in the design and preparation of traditional cloth wares in Southeast Asia, especially in the production of batik fabrics. See JDC, 305.

152   See the glossary (*bezoar*).

153   CMJ, 282.

thing positive about Patani:[154]

> "The factory at Patani should be moved, for no goods are produced there, pepper is imported there from Jambi[155] and Indragiri and other places on the island of Sumatra, although a small quantity of pepper does grow at Patani itself. The people are friendly, but because there is no king, the mandarins, or orang kaya, do as they please. They do not wish to have a king, in order to keep their government as it is; for with their queen they do as they please. There is no law or justice there; indeed, our capital is not safe there, and if the Company could make five cents' profit, the orang kaya will come and forbid our trade, saying that the queen needs the goods, and once we have bought them we have to give them a profit on them. In short, as far as trade is concerned we are treated like slaves there, and there is no end or bound to the presents we have to give to all the unscrupulous mandarins, or orang kaya, because there are so many of them."

A similarly negative tone regarding business in Patani is echoed in another one of his documents:[156]

> "Our people at Patani are not very useful either, for we are vexed too much by the mandarins there and are not allowed to trade there. We have not achieved much either, for in two years' time we only got about 30 *lasts* of goods,[157] while we keep such

---

154 CMJ, 289.
155 River, polity, and settlement located in central-eastern Sumatra. Jambi was second to Aceh as a trading center for pepper during the late 16th and early 17th centuries. See the illustration, 133 and JDC, 364.
156 CMJ, 249.
157 A Dutch unit to measure the weight or volume of ships' cargo, here about 60 tons. See also CJM, 492-3.

an expensive factory there including the many presents we are giving, so that the goods cost us 100 per
cent too much. There is nothing there which is of
any use to us, for pepper we will get at Banten and
Johor, as much as we need. We do not trade with
the Chinese there, since they bring no merchandise
which is useful to us."

Matelieff's verdict on the pepper trade was that the
VOC should focus on other procurement sources and close
the factories at Patani and Aceh:[158]

"So I conclude that, as far as pepper is concerned,
Jeyakerta and Banten with the addition of Johor
should bring us enough pepper for the time being,
without our having to keep a factory at Aceh and
Patani for that purpose."[159]

A few paragraphs earlier, I wrote "For the time being
at least, Matelieff favored Johor over Patani." Matelieff's positive outlook on Batu Sawar was not to last. As a Company
whose resources were being squeezed by large fixed costs
and infrastructure spending, the VOC factory at Batu Sawar
could not justify its overheads. The profits, in other words,
did not actually cover the costs of maintaining the operations there. Matelieff explained:[160]

"The Johor factory: as far as trade is concerned, I
cannot think of a reason why it is profitable for us to
keep an office for the Company there, for no goods

---

158   CMJ, 282.
159   In a letter by Admiral Van Caerden to the Gentlemen Sev-
      enteen, dated 9 January, 1608, he quoted Matelieff as having
      claimed that there "is not much to do", that is there is little
      business at the Dutch factories in Patani, Aceh, and Gresik. See
      De Booy, *Derde Reis*, II, 136.
160   CMJ, 290.

Overleaf: Hand-drawn chart of the Indonesian Archipelago and the South China Sea dating from 1742. The Hague: National Archives of the Netherlands, 4.VEL 346.

whatsoever are produced there. So far all that was loaded on board there was a bit of pepper, which would find its way to Java in any case. But seeing how things stand in the war, one might retain the factory there a bit longer. This is also a location for trade by private merchants, [but] it does not cover the expenses."

The admiral had moved from seeing Johor as a principal supplier of pepper to one that was relatively insignificant. Like Patani, Batu Sawar also relied on pepper imports from Jambi, Indragiri and probably also Siak to sustain the marketplace. Perhaps there were politically-motivated supply bottlenecks, and the sources of production on Sumatra were now delivering their harvests elsewhere. We also know from Matelieff that unlike the case of cloves, nutmeg and mace, pepper saw a steadily growing supply on the market, to the extent that total production is reported to have doubled on Sumatra and around the Straits in the one and a half decades between 1595 and about 1610.[161] In a letter dated 3 May, 1615, Matelieff privately reported to Grotius that in that year alone, Banten was set to export 200,000 bags of pepper weighing 56 pounds each—which amounts to around 5,260 metric tons.[162] The volumes sold here dwarfed the supplies at Batu Sawar. The price of pepper was falling due to this ever-growing supply entering the market.

As a supplier of pepper, Johor may very well have declined due to the political disturbances at the Batu Sawar court or even among its dependencies and allies on Sumatra.

---

161   CMJ, 319.
162   CMJ, 363, 369.

BORNEO.

Duytsche Mylen Vyftien voor een Graedt

Æquinoctiael

Sumatra

IAVA

The Acehnese Empire had, with the accession of Iskandar Muda in 1611, entered a new phase of aggressive expansion. But even if available pepper had remained fairly constant, the supply glut, combined with price erosion, meant that the VOC's factory at Batu Sawar would yield little to no profit while trade volumes were steadily growing elsewhere. It is against the backdrop of these market-driven developments, together with the VOC's need to contain costs in Asia, that the Batu Sawar factory's heyday was drawing to a close.

Batu Sawar and the diamond trade

Readers today may be surprised to find rough or unpolished diamonds on the ledgers of the VOC in Johor. While precious woods and tree resins were collected in the forests of the peninsula, Sumatra and the Riau Islands, the diamonds came from Borneo, which was reputed as a source of high-quality diamonds. Rough (or uncut) stones were also sold at Brunei Bay, Sukadana, Sambas and sometimes also at Banjarmasin. The sale of diamonds at Batu Sawar was sufficiently brisk that in 1609, one of the three new members assuming his new duties at the VOC factory was a diamond specialist named Hector Roos.[163]

The aforementioned Jacques de Coutre, himself a jeweler, had a few things to say about the Borneo diamond trade as well. He wrote: "The island abounds in precious stones

---

163   CMJ, 533. See also M.E. van Opstall, *De reis van de vloot van Pieter Willemsz Verhoeff naar Azië, 1607–1612*, (The Hague, Martinus Nijhoff, 1972), I, 255n2. Opstall explained that Roos had arrived in Asia with the fleet of Admiral Verhoeff with the objective of placing him at the factory in Batu Sawar. He left on 26 September, 1610, for Sukadana and one month later transferred to Sambas. He was killed in January 1611 together with Jacob van der Meer and members of the crew on the *Vliegende Draak* (Flying Dragon).

and metals. It has a lot of gold and many diamonds, which can be found in two rivers on the island, one is called Lawai, the other Sukadana, when the water level is low."[164] What De Coutre reveals here is that the diamonds were not mined, but panned in the riverbeds as alluvial deposits during the dry season. This is confirmed by a few additional testimonies from around the same period. One Dutch source mentions that the diamonds were "fished" from the rivers.[165] The Englishman Ralph Fitch, who also wrote around this time, noted: Borneo "is an iland ... [from] whence come the diamants .... And they find them in the rivers; for the king will not suffer them to digge the rocke."[166] The principal source of these diamonds was not the coastal areas, but rather the valleys in the interior in regions known as Landak and Mempawah. Traditionally, the tribal leaders here were loyal to the ruler of Sukadana (who himself was subject to the adipati of Surabaya),[167] but during the first and second decades of the 17th century, the adipati of Sambas (a vassal of Raja Bongsu of Johor) competed with Sukadana for control over these areas. In this endeavor, and with an eye cast on cornering the diamond market in this region, the VOC lent the adipati of Sambas a helping hand by signing a treaty with him in October 1610.[168]

The memorials show that Matelieff was well aware of the potential value of the Borneo diamond trade to the Company, but he also expressed his apprehension and reservations about it. Since this was a compact, high value commodity, he was concerned that dishonest employees would

---

164 CDJ, 148.

165 JO, III, 303.

166 Ralph Fitch *Early Travels in India, 1583-1619*, ed. W. Foster (London: Humphrey Milsford and Oxford University Press, 1921), 42.

167 CDJ, 580.

168 CMJ, 446-8, for an English translation of this treaty.

be tempted to help themselves to these small but valuable gems. Also, because the diamonds tied up a lot of Company capital, errors in judging their quality and value carried a huge risk and were potentially disastrous.[169] Then there was the issue of having local rulers meddle in the market and exploit it to their own advantage. Johor was certainly no exception in this regard:[170]

> "[The king of Johor] ... has a place there, I believe at the river called Sambas, which belongs to Raja Seberang. We would be safe there[171] and we could let the diamonds be brought there from upriver.[172] An argument against this, however, would be that the king of Johor, who is very greedy, would want to shear the sheep and let us shear the pigs.[173] One ought to make a deal with him. If it could be done without involving him, on the other hand, that would be more profitable, but less safe. One should find an occasion to discuss it with him and see what his inclinations are in this matter. Without that, I cannot make a definitive assessment ..."

Factious court politics

The difficulties with the diamond business identified by Matelieff are typical of the challenges and perils of doing business in Southeast Asia at the turn of the 16th and 17th centuries. If it was already so difficult dealing with a party that was enthusiastically favorable to one's cause, what

---

169   CMJ, 295, 329.
170   CMJ, 295-6.
171   Read: Sambas; probably located at or around the river estuary.
172   Read: the Sambas River and its tributaries.
173   Read: the king of Johor takes the lion's share of the profits and leaves slim pickings for the Dutch.

about rulers who were lukewarm or even suspicious? The situation in the Indonesian Archipelago was rendered more challenging because in sharp contrast to the situation in Europe where no nobleman would want to be seen dabbling in trade, royalty and the nobility were in fact proactively engaged in commerce. If the nobility in Europe derived its status from feudal land tenure, royalty in the Malay polities sustained their status through patronage and the redistribution of material goods. Foreign goods, their accumulation at the court and their redistribution to the Malay elites acted as a powerful source of political legitimacy.[174] Thus, Southeast Asian monarchs were less concerned with establishing a unified bureaucratic administration (which was a western priority or preoccupation in the late early modern period) than with maintaining ritual and ceremony, retaining the capacity to elevate members of the court to social rank, as well as dispensing material or symbolic rewards.[175]

It was not unheard of that "kings" on Sumatra and the Malay Peninsula acted as the biggest, or the sole merchant in their polity.[176] Thus, while foreign merchants

---

174   See for example Oliver W. Wolters, *History, Culture and Region in Southeast Asian Perspectives* (Singapore: ISEAS, 1999), 43-4; Tony Day, *Fluid Iron. State Formation in Southeast Asia* (Honolulu: Hawai'i University Press, 2002), esp. 12-13.

175   Kenneth R. Hall, "Upstream and Downstream Unification in Southeast Asia's First Islamic Polity: The Changing Sense of Community in the Fifteenth Century 'Hikayat Raja-Raja Pasai' Court Chronicle," *Journal of the Economic and Social History of the Orient*, 44.2 (2001): 198-229, esp. 208; Anthony Milner, *Kerajaan: Malay Political Culture on the Eve of Colonial Rule* (Tucson: University of Arizona Press, 1982).

176   For a specific example of this period, see JDC, 81. For this observation, see Milner, *The Malays* (Oxford: Wiley-Blackwell, 2008), 72; also Milner, Kerajaan, 23; See also John Crawfurd, *History of the Indian Archipelago*, facsimile edition printed by Archibald Constable & Co., Edinburgh, 1820, 3 vols. (London: Frank Cass, 1967), III, 152, "A Malay prince is, therefore, as

were encouraged to visit their ports, they were effectively restricted to trading with a single—or a very limited number—of local counter-parties. In this way, rulers and their leading nobles became merchant-officials who used trade as an instrument of redistributive patronage and therewith sustained their legitimacy and maintained their supporters at court—and beyond.

The presence of powerful merchant-officials such as the bendahara, laksamana, shahbandar, or temenggong, combined with the patronage wielded by members of the royal family, contributed significantly to the multi-polarity of pre-modern Malay polities. Early 17th century Johor is a case in point: power focused on the four surviving sons of Raja Ali Jalla bin Abdul Jalil as well as the Johor bendahara, Sri Paduka Raja, Tun Sri Lanang. Matelieff's writings serve as a who's who of early 17th century Johor court politics. It would appear that he may have personally met at least three of the four brothers and of course the bendahara. How he sized them up and ultimately judged them evidently revolved around twin criteria: their abilities and their European loyalties. Did they support the Dutch or were they in the pocket of the Portuguese?

Some readers may be surprised to learn that, on the whole, the Johorese were doing brisk business with the Portuguese from Melaka at the turn of the 16th and 17th centuries. The study of Paulo Pinto, *The Portuguese in the Straits of Melaka*, confirms as much.[177] Relations between Johor and Melaka were admittedly patchy, occasionally tense

---

already mentioned, in general the first and often the only merchant in his country"; A.P. Rubin, "The Use of Piracy in Malayan Waters," in *Grotian Society Papers 1968. Studies in the History of the Law of Nations*, ed. Charles H. Alexandrowicz (The Hague: Martinus Nijhoff, 1970), 123, including ibid n. 63.

177   P.J. de Sousa Pinto, *The Portuguese and the Straits of Melaka, 1575-1619. Power, Trade and Diplomacy* (Singapore: NUS Press, 2012).

and sometimes even openly hostile. The latter was notably the case after Raja Bongsu had entered into friendly relations with Jacob van Heemskerck in 1603. But there can be little doubt: in Johor there were deep commercial interests on both sides, on the part of both the Johorese merchant-officials as well as the Portuguese. And the Dutch were now trying to get their proverbial foot into the door. It should hardly surprise that Matelieff made the distinction he did: Who is on which side? Portuguese or Dutch? Do they side with our enemy or with us? The problem with these two opposites is that they do not leave room for anything inbetween. In other words, a Johorese noble who did not come out strongly in favor of the Dutch side was likely to be branded a Portuguese sympathizer.

Matelieff's writings paint a problematic picture in this regard. We are already familiar with two of the sons of the late Raja Ali Jalla: Raja Bongsu (alias Raja Seberang or Raja di Ilir) and Raja Laut. Raja Bongsu, the youngest of the brothers, is quite clearly the star and the darling of the Dutch— from Heemskerck to Matelieff and Verhoeff. That should not surprise for Raja Bongsu was the most outspoken supporter of the Dutch at the Batu Sawar court. He was described as a capable and focused young man in his early to mid-30s with a glowing charisma.[178] Only in one instance did Matelieff employ a negative attribute to describe Raja Bongsu, when he called him "greedy". The latter acted and signed himself as co-ruler of Johor, but the admiral had detected some tension or jealousy between Raja Bongsu and his older half-brother and co-ruler Ala'udin. He was reportedly married to one of Ala'udin's daughters. We can further glean from the writings at hand that Raja Bongsu had his own pockets of supporters, his *negeri*,[179] first at Kota Seberang located not

---

178   See the description below, p. 94-5, and Document 12.

179   CMJ, 497-8. In its most basic meaning, this Malay term means "settlement", either large or small. The Malay expression *isi*

far away from Batu Sawar, and also at Sambas on the great island of Borneo. The admiral, however, was well aware that Raja Bongsu's power at the court was limited, for in his letter to Paul van Caerden dated 4 January, 1608, he noted:[180]

"... Raja Seberang has no power, he dare not command the noblemen, the noblemen do not want them as their king, for then they would not have so much power as they do now; so things stay in between."

Raja Bongsu, in sum, was capable and likable; he was a supporter of the Dutch, but evidently politically weak and lacked broad support at court.

His half-brother Raja Laut has, of course, already been mentioned in an earlier section of this introduction. To sum up the situation: Raja Laut was probably the bearer of several titles or honorifics, including shahbandar, Raja Negara, *ketua orang laut* and possibly also laksamana. He was himself almost certainly of orang laut descent. His exact identity remains hazy, but the short description we have of him in the *Journal* is nothing less than hair-raising.[181] Needless to say, Raja Laut did not leave a positive impression with our admiral. And whom did he side with? The Portuguese—well at least that is what Matelieff claimed.

---

negeri simply means "the population", and consequently, the "substance" of the *negeri* are neither land nor (royal) institutions or officials, but simply the people. Admittedly, however, the term has been translated in many instances as "state" or "polity", but this is not always correct, and appears to be a usage adopted only in the 19th century. See A.C. Milner, *The Invention of Politics in Colonial Malaya*, 104; Milner, *The Malays* (Oxford: Wiley-Blackwell, 2008), 59; J.M. Gullick, *Indigenous Political Systems of Western Malaya* (London: The Athlone Press, 1958), 21.

180   CMJ, 235.

181   CMJ, 154; see also above, p. 136.

Matelieff also does not have kind words about the ruling monarch: Ala'udin Ri'ayat Shah III. Matelieff described the king as a serious alcoholic and a womanizer, who did have his lucid moments. (More about that episode later.) For now, the most substantive comment about King Ala'udin is found in the *Journal*. It states: [182]

"The eldest [son of Raja Ali Jalla] now rules over the Malays and is called Yang di Pertuan, but that seems to be his title rather than his name. ... The Yang di Pertuan is a person of little activity. He is used to sleeping until it is almost noon; then he eats and washes and proceeds to get drunk, so that he is impossible to deal with after noon, for one has to drink with him and do drunkards' things. He does not trouble himself with anything, leaving everything to the noblemen and Raja Seberang. He does not want to hear about any difficulties, and if one urges him to do something—mustering men or things like that—he simply remains silent; and if one asks him two or three times, it is all the same. To sum up, there is nothing he is less capable of than being a king. He does not think of his kingdom or his subjects, as long as he has wine and women."

Matelieff, we are informed, had been briefed about King Ala'udin's character and disposition by the surviving members of Johor's embassy to the Dutch Republic who had returned home aboard Matelieff's flagship. A memorial explains:[183]

"The admiral knew only what the envoys who had come with him from Holland had [already] told him: that Raja Seberang managed everything, while the great king did not occupy himself with any-

---

182   CMJ, 153.
183   CMJ, 166.

thing but women and drinking—which the admiral found to be true from his own experience, so that he did not worry. …. Sometimes [King Ala'udin] was asleep, sometimes he was eating, sometimes he was drunk, so that it was practically never a good time to speak with him."

The materials at hand paint a decidedly mixed picture about Ala'udin's European loyalties. The *Journal*, for example, claims that "the king did not want peace with the Portuguese, because he found no reliability in them, only deceit." But Ala'udin's attitudes toward the Dutch was hardly different. Matelieff, we are informed, was "surprised that the king thought so little of the alliance with the Dutch". But none of this seems very conclusive, as there are also sources attesting to his pro-Portuguese credentials, among them the 17th century Portuguese author, Manuel Godinho de Erédia, and in the 20th century, Carl-Alexander Gibson-Hill.[184]

The fourth brother is a man referred to in the *Journal* as Raja Siak. Although his precise identity is somewhat murky, he is thought to have been the main champion of the Portuguese cause at the Johor royal court. The *Journal* claims that he was "married to [the queen of] Patani's daughter" and that he was a "man of little activity and not blessed with any kingly virtues, but a naive fool".[185] The statement: "He always stays within Siak and rarely goes to Johor" may account for the principal reason why Matelieff's knowledge of him was vague. The *Journal* may have only been reporting from hearsay, and Raja Siak may have not been present at Batu Sawar at the time of the admiral's visit to the court in August and September of 1606. The Dutch academic Pieter Gerritsz.

---

184   See Erédia, *Declaraçam de Malaca,* fol. 44 verso; PSMS, 107; and Carl-Alexander Gibson-Hill, "The Alleged Death of Sultan Ala'udin of Johor at Acheh in 1613," *JMBRAS* 291 (1956): 130, 138.

185   CMJ, 153.

Rouffaer claims that the individual in question is known from the *Sejarah Melayu* (Malay Annals) as Raja Hasan of Siak. Elisa Netscher, in his book *De Nederlanders in Djohor en Siak* (The Dutch in Johor and Siak), identified Raja Siak as an illegitimate brother of Raja Bongsu. However a 17th century English text, the *Standish-Croft Journal*, claims that Raja Siak was an in-law and not a sibling or half-brother of the other three princes. It is further unclear whether it was Raja Siak whose ill-fated marriage to the queen of Patani's daughter is described in Raja Bongsu's and King Ala'udin's letter to the king of Holland of February, 1609.[186]

Aside from the four sons of the late Raja Ali Jalla who are, with the notable exception of Raja Bongsu, supposedly all avid supporters of the Portuguese, there are of course the other high-ranking nobles and merchant-officials of Johor. Matelieff has few words to lose about them, other than the claim that they are all in the pocket of the Portuguese: "The bendahara and laksamana are pro-Portuguese and none of the great king's noblemen can be counted on" and "the orang kaya favor the Portuguese".[187] But then again, the *Journal* observed in the context of Matelieff's visit to Batu Sawar that "the nobility did not seem at all inclined to make peace with the Portuguese".[188] The laksamana may have been identical to the shahbandar of Singapore and Sri Raja Negara, as has been previously highlighted, but what about the bendahara?

The issue at hand is admittedly a sensitive one—not simply because the bendahara allegedly supported the Portuguese—but rather because of the identity of the benda-

---

186 CMJ, 509-10; W. Foster, ed., *The Voyage of Thomas Best to the East Indies 1612-1614* (London: Hakluyt Society, 1934), 169; E. Netscher, *De Nederlanders in Djohor en Siak* (Batavia: Bruining & Wijt, 1870), 29, On the definitive linkage of Raja Siak with Hasan, see RWME, 445n1.

187 CMJ, 194n278, 235.

188 CMJ, 198, and below, 118.

hara in question: Tun Sri Lanang. He is of course intimately connected to one of the most important works of Malay literature, namely the *Sulalat-us-salatin*, better known today as the *Sejarah Melayu*.[189] The snippets of information we can glean from our eyewitness reports are what they are, and they attest to a view of Tun Sri Lanang that can hardly be reconciled with today's image of him. I shall let the passage speak for itself and let readers make their own judgment. The context of the following excerpt are the discussions leading up to the joint Johor-Dutch attack on Melaka in May 1606. The bendahara is said to have noted that the Dutch had easily taken Ternate and Ambon[190] in 1605 without any help from local forces, so he wondered aloud why the Dutch were now not able to accomplish the same in the case of Melaka. The high point comes with the bendahara's words that "he had not come to fight, but to watch the fight".[191] Matelieff became irritated with the bendahara, because he had arrived with his fleet to fight the Portuguese at the expressed request of the Johor rulers. It would also appear that King Ala'udin—in an unexpected moment of sobriety—also became annoyed and put the bendahara in his place. The bendahara's supposed Portuguese sympathies were squarely blamed for this audacious behavior:[192]

---

189   See Borschberg, "Left Holding the Bag. The Johor-VOC Alliance and the Twelve Years' Truce (1606-1613)" in *The Twelve Years Truce (1609). Peace, Truce War and Law in the Low Countries at the Turn of the 17th Century*, ed. R. Lesaffer (Leiden: Brill-Nijhoff, 2014), 89-120.

190   Island and port city located in the Malukus, and a trading post of importance for the spice trade (cloves, nutmeg, mace). The town of Ambon traces its origin to a settlement located outside the walls of the late 16th century Portuguese fortress. The town and island of Ambon fell to the Dutch in 1605. See the illustration, 111 and CMJ, 527; JDC, 251.

191   CMJ, 168.

192   CMJ, 168.

"The bendahara even had the audacity to say to the admiral, in King [Ala'udin's] presence while he was in his council, that our people had conquered Ternate and Ambon without the inhabitants' help, and therefore they ought to do so in this case as well; for he had not come to fight, but to watch the fight. To which the admiral replied: 'I have come here as a servant to the king, the Yang di Pertuan, whose war this is. And if you do not wish to be his servant, nor do him any service, you can say so; and if the king, Yang di Pertuan, commands me to, I will make such people leave here.' When the king heard this, he was annoyed with the bendahara, and many noblemen were very pleased that the admiral spoke to him like that, since he was an arrogant fool and a rude beast, who seemed to be more on the Portuguese than on the Dutch side. [The bendahara's] position was that of the king's governor."

Matelieff's value to historians of Singapore and the region

So why should someone interested in the history of Singapore and Johor read the writings of Admiral Matelieff? What are the main insights and how do they impact the way we understand Singapore and the Straits region in the period before 1800?

The texts, all originally written in Dutch, endorse a growing consensus that for much of the early modern period, and especially during the late 16th and early 17th centuries, Singapore was not a backwater or neglected place forgotten by time. It was in fact, quite the opposite. There are four principal insights a reader can take away from scrutinizing this book:

First, at the turn of the 16th and 17th centuries, Singapore was home to a port and a shahbandar. The official who maintained his residence on the island was the leader of the orang laut communities around the Straits and the islands. Given the role of these nomadic sea tribes in manning the Johor navy, it is likely that the shahbandar of Singapore also concurrently fulfilled the role as laksamana or admiral. Singapore would have been home to the Johorese armada.

Second, Singapore was seen to be an island located within a larger estuary dominated by the Johor River. Understood in this way, Singapore was deemed by the early colonial powers as one of several port towns spanning the Johor River and should therefore be considered to have been an integral part of its riverine economy. The other main ports along the river included Johor Lama, Kota Seberang and the capital city Batu Sawar.

Third, "Johor" has been described in early European colonial sources as one of the main pepper ports of Southeast Asia. It is mentioned alongside other key emporia such as Aceh, Kedah, Patani and Banten. In the minds of European merchants, the name "Johor" refers first and foremost to the royal administrative center at Batu Sawar, but not exclusively so. As a result, the name Johor can also include some or all of the principal riverine towns that were engaged in commerce, such as notably Johor Lama and Singapore, both of which were home to a resident shahbandar. Johor is reported to have been a thriving commercial center in the early 17th century, acting not only as a principal outlet for pepper brought in from Sumatra, but also for jungle produce, odoriferous woods, tree resins, unminted gold and precious stones. In the period under review, Batu Sawar was home to a factory of the Dutch East India Company (VOC).

Fourth and finally, the writings of Matelieff help answer one of the most important questions concerning Singapore history in the early modern period, namely: Why did the island—or the region as a whole—remain unrecognized for so long despite its strategic location and importance within

Johor's thriving commerce? The answer, put simply, was that Singapore and the region around the Johor River estuary were most certainly recognized for their geo-strategic potential. For this reason, local rulers and the early colonial powers competed with each other for control of the Straits and the river estuary during the first half of the 17th century. We are aware of plans both on the parts of the Portuguese and Spanish as well as the Dutch to build fortifications on what would now be the sovereign territory of Singapore, specifically on the northwestern tip of present-day Sentosa. The purpose of this fortification was to monitor and control all maritime traffic passing between the Melaka Straits and the Bay of Bengal in the west toward the South China Sea and additional destinations around the Indonesian Archipelago in the east. In order to improve the way the VOC did business in Asia, Admiral Matelieff had proposed the selection of an optimally located site where the Dutch could establish a central base in Southeast Asia.

Of the six locations that were seriously considered at some stage, Singapore and the Johor River estuary region featured prominently. On the advice of Admiral Matelieff and others, however, the Dutch decided not to establish their main base in or around the Singapore Straits region. Court politics in Johor were seen to be unpredictable and unstable; food was scarce and had to be imported from as far away as Java, Makassar, Pegu (Burma) and Bengal; and in the age of sail, the physical geography of the region meant that ships could not optimally exploit the monsoon winds for long distance trade. In contrast to the Sunda Strait, which Matelieff claimed could be accessed and navigated all year round, the Singapore and Melaka Straits could not. Delays in ship arrivals and departures from Europe or within Asia meant higher costs to the VOC, and for the entire lifespan of the Dutch Company, costs had to be contained as much as possible. For these and related considerations, Matelieff and the Gentlemen Directors in Amsterdam moved their focus southwards to Java with huge consequences for the historic development of the Company and the region at large.

Singapore and the Johor River region may very well have been recognized as a strategically important nodal point in the maritime traffic connecting East and West. When considered against the backdrop of other factors such as available food supplies and operational efficiency of the Company, however, the region was deemed at best a reasonable second choice. That is to say: the Dutch certainly recognized it, but chose not to take advantage of it because there were better opportunities elsewhere.

Document 1

Excerpts from the Journal of Admiral Matelieff's Voyage to Asia, 1605-1608

[The following passage has been excerpted from the *Historische Verhael* (Historical Narrative) of the Voyage of Admiral Matelieff to the East Indies published in Isaac Commelin's *Begin ende Voortgang* (Beginning and Continuation) in 1645/6. Having left the Dutch Republic in May 1605, the 11 ships and 1,440 mates under the supreme command of Admiral Matelieff rounded the Cape of Good Hope and reached the island of Mauritius in the final weeks of 1605. Here, Matelieff exchanged information with Admiral Steven van der Hagen, the first VOC fleet commander, who was on his return voyage to Europe. After a month, Matelieff set sail again, passed the Nicobar Islands and reached the western coast of the Malay peninsula toward the end of April 1606. Messengers were set ashore to rush to the capital Batu Sawar and inform the king of Johor that the Dutch fleet had arrived. The excerpt begins about a week later, with the arrival of the shahbandar of Singapore who had been sent to reconnoiter the situation firsthand.]

The Shahbandar of Singapore comes to inspect Admiral Matelieff's fleet

... On the fifth of that month [of May, 1606], some entrenchment baskets were brought to Pulau Melaka from

Glazed tile painting in Lisbon of a Portuguese-style foist of the mid-16th century. Peter Borschberg, private collection.

Pulau Besar.[193] Toward the evening, two *perahus*[194] from Johor joined the fleet; the King [of Johor, Ala'udin Ri'ayat

---

193   Two islets located in the Straits close to Melaka.

194   A type of small craft that can be either sailed or rowed. The term is very elastic in its application, and vessel types covered by this category range from coastal cargo ships (that are chiefly sailed) to longboats on a river. See JDC, 334-5; SMS, 334.

Shah III] had dispatched them from there[195] five days earlier. The commander was the shahbandar of Singapore, called Sri Raja Negara. Admiral [Matelieff] welcomed them as they were coming from the king of Johor, our ally, and let them navigate through the fleet and view the ships. They told him that the king had sent them to see if there were ships from Holland, because he had received a message from Perak[196] that some ships had sailed to Melaka which were thought to be Dutch. They said that they had seen the yacht[197] we had sent more than halfway [from] Johor three days earlier, and that as soon as the king was advised of our coming, he would come immediately. One could well expect him within eight days with 20 galleys[198] and 30 foists.[199] After this, they wanted to leave right away, which they did on that same night. They also knew about the armada from Goa,[200] and that the viceroy in person was on it.

On 6 May, two perahus full of people came rowing to the city from south of the battery, and they could not be stopped. In the afternoon, another large perahu full of people was rowed away from the city unhindered. To pre-

---

195   The author of the *Journal* evidently has a specific location in mind which is unfortunately not revealed.

196   River, port and polity situated in the central-western region of the Malay Peninsula. Perak was chiefly known in the early modern period as a supplier of tin.

197   A sailing vessel similar to a sloop favored by the VOC in the early 17th century. As a rule, the yacht featured a single mast with lateen (triangular) sails, more than one lateen headsail and usually equipped with oars.

198   A type of vessel that is predominantly rowed but also aided by sail that traces its origins to ancient Greece and Rome. See also JDC, 323; SMS, 333.

199   A type of vessel that normally featured a single row of oars and a single mast. See JDC, 321; SMS, 332, and the illustration, 106.

200   The capital and center of Portuguese India, located on the central-western coastal region of India.

vent this from happening again, the *Groote Sonne's*[201] yacht and the *Middelburg's* big sloop,[202] together with the *Swarte Leeuw's*[203] boat, were ordered to anchor there. Nonetheless, two small perahus came from the outside during the aforementioned watch, and no sooner had these been sighted than two foists and some more perahus full of people came rowing to the city. Despite our people's efforts, they reached the city unharmed. Those inside celebrated a great triumph over it, because they had been given relief. These foists had been sent on an embassy to Pahang[204] some time before, in order to rescue some Portuguese who had been on a stranded ship. As a result, 80 white Portuguese and over 100 blacks now came into the city, so that they became twice as strong as they had been.

Johor promises help in the Dutch campaign against Portuguese Melaka

On 13 May [1606], the sloop returned from Johor, bringing news that the king was to follow within four days with as many men as he could muster. He had already sent messengers through all his land to gather men and ammuni-

---

201   Lit. "Great Sun", one of the ships of Matelieff's fleet. CMJ, 102n376.

202   A single-mast sailing boat featuring a lateen mainsail and a headsail. See CMJ, 515; JDC, 343.

203   Lit. "Black Lion", one of the ships of Matelieff's fleet. See CMJ, 151n62.

204   Polity, port and river located in southeastern peninsular Malaysia. In the late 16th and early 17th centuries, Pahang was considered as a "vassal" or client state of Johor. It was famous chiefly for its pepper, gold dust (panned from the river beds) and bezoar stones. It was also important on account of the riverine trading network that linked to two coastal towns of Pahang (east) and Muar (west). See CMJ, 566; JDC, 372-3.

tion. On the 14th, the admiral was handed a letter from the king of Johor which had been translated into our language by the Dutch living there and signed by him. It stated the following:

> The King of Johor, called Raja Seberang (which means 'king of the other side'), wishes the admiral good luck and success in that which he has planned. You (i.e. the Lord Admiral) who have been sent here by the king of Holland[205] to fight our and your enemies, undoubtedly your name and fame will deserve to be spread around the whole world, because you are not afraid to stand up against the tyranny of the Portuguese in this country as well as in your own. I deem myself fortunate to have met the men you sent, Lodewijk Isacksen and Hans van Hagen, who notified me of your arrival at Melaka—indeed, who came to redeem our poor people from Portuguese slavery. The service your king has rendered to my unworthy person will be recompensed by the present messenger to those whom your king has sent here, in accordance with my meagre resources. No king on earth could render me such a service as your king already has. I send you Encik Amar with Encik Kamar[206] to advise you of my coming, God willing. I am expecting my rowers and will not be slow in coming, once they have arrived; indeed, if I had two galleys ready, I would come immediately.[207]

---

205   An expression commonly used in correspondence by Asian rulers in their correspondence with either the Stadholder or the States General. See also the glossary for an explanation (*King of Holland*).

206   These were surviving members of Johor's embassy to the Dutch Republic, 1603-5. See also above, 56, 64, 152.

207   According to the printed text of the *Journal*, Raja Bongsu arrived on 17 May 1606, with his 300 men, the same day the Johor royals concluded a first formal treaty with Admiral Matelieff.

Portrait of Steven van der Hagen by P.M.A. Schouman, 1720-1792. Rijksmuseum Amsterdam, RP-T-00-1284.

I expect many bantins[208] and will send them as soon as possible. I am keeping your envoys Lodewijk Isacksen and Hans van Hagen with me, they will come aboard my galley with me and thus arrive together with me to help organize the enterprise. His Excellency has honored me so greatly that I cannot requite. Furthermore I am so much indebted to you and all those who were sent to liberate us that I can never repay it, since we are a poor people.

On 17 May, the admiral received the message that the king of Johor was already at the ships with his galleys and foists in which he could have around 300 men in all, most of them slaves. It was Raja Bongsu, or Raja Seberang, the same who had sent the envoys to Holland with the presents for His Excellency, [Stadholder Prince Maurice].

Description of the four sons of Raja Ali Jalla bin Abdul Jalil

In order to understand his situation, one should know that the old king of Johor, [Raja Ali Jalla bin Abdul Jalil], who was a good warrior and was often at war with the Portuguese, left four sons.[209] The eldest now rules over the Malays and is called Yang di Pertuan,[210] but that seems to be his title rather than his name. By another woman he

---

208 A Malay craft often used in the 16th and 17th centuries in naval warfare. It was propelled by breast oars and featured two rudders and two masts. See JDC, 304; SMS, 331.

209 Another translation of this section in GPFT, appendix 13, 211–5.

210 The Malay title for king or ruler. See CMJ, 525.

had Raja Siak, which means "king of Siak"; Siak is a fief of the crown of Johor. He married [the queen[211] of] Patani's[212] daughter and is a man of little activity and not blessed with any kingly virtues, but a bad blood; he always stays within Siak and rarely goes to Johor. The Yang di Pertuan is equally a person of little activity, used to sleeping until it is almost noon; then he eats and washes and proceeds to get drunk, so that he is impossible to deal with after noon. Then one has to drink with him and do drunkards' things. He does not trouble himself with anything, leaving everything to the noblemen and Raja Seberang. He does not want to hear about any difficulties, and if one urges him to do something—mustering men or things like that—he simply remains silent. Even if one asks him two or three times, it is all the same. To sum up, there is nothing he is less capable of than being a king. He does not think of his kingdom or his subjects, as long as he has wine and women.

By his second wife, the king of Johor had Raja Bongsu who is now called Raja Seberang, meaning "king of the other side", because he lives on the opposite side of the [Johor] River from the city of Batu Sawar, where he has a fortress[213] as well, and part of his subjects; but he is a vassal of the Yang di Pertuan. He is about 35 years old, almost white, not very tall, but wise, forgiving, not choleric, and very prudent; an enemy of the Portuguese, industrious in his business, which he would also conduct diligently if he had power. In short, worthy of being king of Johor and Melaka. He would also recognize the help one would spend on him, and in as far as could be judged, he is completely loyal to us. He always respects his brother, the Yang di Pertuan, who loves him

---

211   The queen in question was Raja Hijau. See also the list of place names *(Patani)*.

212   Port and polity on the Isthmus of Kra facing the Gulf of Siam.

213   Raja Bongsu's dependency on the opposite river bank was known as Kota Seberang.

much as well, but of course the Yang di Pertuan secretly harbors quite a bit of jealousy. From his third wife, [Raja Ali Jalla], the old king of Johor, had a son named Raja Laut that is "king of the sea"—a man capable of nothing but smoking tobacco, drinking arak and chewing betel with it, indeed worthy of being bound hands and feet and sunk into the sea; a big drunkard, killer and fornicator, and everything to do with those three things he knows inside out. All the brothers drink wine, except Raja Seberang, who has never tasted wine[214] or spirits. And as the lord is, such are the noblemen of all these kings.

Negotiating the Johor-Dutch treaty of May 1606

The admiral went to meet this Raja Bongsu or Seberang with yachts and boats and honored him by firing a salute. They proceeded to welcome each other, and the king[215] presented the admiral with a golden kris,[216] inlaid with some stones of little value. After a meal had been held on board, they began discussing their business, for the admiral did not want to go ashore without first knowing where he stood, and what help the king would provide during the siege, so that he could base his plans on it.

But when they started to talk about help, they could

---

214 Here to be understood as alcohol in general.

215 The word in the original Dutch text, *koning*, translates as "king", but it is not exactly clear which king the author (Abraham van den Broeck?) has in mind here: Raja Bongsu or the Yang di Pertuan, Ala'udin. Here and in subsequence instances, the original word has been left standing, and it is assumed that the "king" in question is most likely Raja Bongsu.

216 A Malay (ceremonial) dagger. Erédia describes it as a dagger featuring a blade measuring about 55 centimeters in length, is "made of a fine steel" and "bears a deadly poison. The sheath is of wood, the hilt is of animals' horn or a rare stone, or of gold and precious gems." See CMJ, 488; JDC, 326; MGED, 31-2.

not get anything else or anything certain from him other than that he was a poor king with little power, but he would do whatever he could, and people would keep coming. He did not know what his brother would contribute. In short, no matter how the admiral talked and discoursed, there was no knowing what aid [the king] would give in the coming siege—he kept repeating that he was a poor king and that was why he had written to the king of Holland for help against the Portuguese: if he were powerful enough on his own, he would not have called on ours, and so on. So in the end, the admiral had to stop talking about [the king's] assistance and continue on the topic of the treaty between the two of them.

After long protestations as to who would make his demands first, the admiral even had to give into [the king] and make his demands, stating that he wanted the city in order to conduct trade, store his goods, and to occupy it with Dutch [settlers]. The king was to have all of the country [outside the city], and they would help each other like brothers against all enemies in defensive [war] and against the Portuguese and Spanish [also] in offensive war. To this the king replied that if he was not to have the city, why would he want to take it from the hands of the Portuguese? As to the countryside, he did not care, he had 20 times more land than he could fill with subjects. Furthermore, this could not be called help, but merely a change from a worse to a better situation, and even that could turn out differently over time if our people were like the Portuguese, something he could not be certain of. In that case, it could not be said that we came to his aid, but that he came to ours, to give his own land to a party more unknown than the one who had it now, merely in the hope of better neighborliness. Whether this was right and fair, our people could judge for themselves, who wanted the reputation of coveting no one's property and always complained about the injustice done to them by the Portuguese, bearing arms against them as well for that reason.

The admiral, in turn, asked what reward for fighting our men would receive then, once they had helped him. [The king] replied that he wanted to give them space to build a house where they could bring all their wares free of toll. The admiral replied that that would not be freedom which was really worth anything, for our people had little to bring to his country, and a place to build a house he would give to his enemies too, to further trade in his country; just as the kings of Aceh, Banten,[217] and Ternate[218] gave it to us, without any service to them from us. [The admiral] finally added that he had not asked for the king's property because the city as it is now had not been built by his ancestors, it was all the work of the Portuguese; so that our people would only enjoy from him an area of land as big as the city of Melaka, for what was on it belonged neither to him nor to his ancestors.

The Johor-Dutch treaty of 17 May, 1606

When the king noticed, after much talking and replying, that he could not have the city and was getting nowhere, he said that he was content to leave the city to the admiral, if he were to grant him a request. To this, the admiral replied that if it was in his power and if it was based on reason, he wanted to accommodate him. The king then took the admiral and the interpreter apart and whispered into their ears that he asked that an expedition to Aceh be made with him, to drive out its king.[219] But the admiral said that that was not reasonable, because our people were at peace with Aceh; he

---

217   Port and polity in west Java near the Sunda Strait. See CMJ, 532; JDC, 352.

218   Clove-producing island and polity of the Malukus. See CMJ, 557, 583; JDC, 352.

219   Ali Ri'ayat Shah of Aceh ruled briefly between 1604 and 1607. He was succeeded by the great Iskandar Muda under whom the Acehnese empire reached the height of its territorial expanse.

did want to promise him that ours would help protect him with all their might if the king of Aceh[220] came to make war on him, or rather that they would do their best to make a peace between the two kings. At last they agreed with one another and made the following contract, which was written down in [both] Dutch and in Malay and then signed and sworn to by both kings before Melaka. It stated the following:

> Agreement between Admiral Cornelis Matelieff de Jonge, in the name of the High Mighty Gentlemen States General of the United Netherlands[221] on the one hand, and the illustrious and mighty king of Johor on the other, on 17 May 1606, on the ship *Oranje*,[222] anchored in the roadstead of Melaka.[223]

> 1. The admiral promises, in the name as mentioned above, at the request of the king, to help him take the city of Melaka from the hands of the Portuguese, enemies to them both. Each will employ his utmost powers to drive them out of it. This exploit having been brought about with God's help, the walled city as it is now within its walls will remain forever in free ownership of the aforementioned Gentlemen States without any tax or acknowledgment of authority. The aforementioned king hereby gives this as a reward for fighting. The entire country will remain subject to His Majesty, on the understanding that if the aforementioned

---

220 Ali Ri'ayat Shah with whom Matelieff's deputy, Vice-Admiral Olivier de Vivere, signed a treaty in January 1607. For an English translation of this agreement, see CMJ, 397-9.

221 The federal assembly of the Dutch Republic comprising delegates of the seven provinces. See also CMJ, 482.

222 This was Admiral Matelieff's flagship, see CMJ, 146n30.

223 This treaty evidently served later as a model for the one signed between Vice-Admiral de Vivere and Ali Ri'ayat Shah of Aceh.

Gentlemen States or their captain wish to fortify the city, they will be allowed to take as much land to it as they will see fit.

2.   The aforementioned Gentlemen States will be able to fetch and cut wood from all the king's land in order to build ships and for the needs of the city.

3.   All the vassals of the aforementioned Gentlemen States will be allowed to unload their ships and goods, regardless of the place from which they come, including hired ships, junks[224] and pera-hus, in the aforementioned city; the king will have no authority in this matter and will not levy any tolls on it, in or out.

4.   The king will not tolerate that any Dutchmen,[225] European nations or their descendants conduct trade in any of his lands, unless they have a written authorization from the Governor of Melaka. If they do not, they will be persecuted and arrested as enemies.

5.   On the other hand, His Majesty will populate

---

224   A type of sailing ship that comes in various sizes, generally featuring a double (wooden) hull, one or several masts, and sails made of cloth or woven reeds. Erédia describes them as "tall boats like freight-bearing carracks, with two rudders and masts and with sails made of woven palm-leaves and of matting, traversed by bamboos at definite intervals, so that they could fold and gather up the sail with despatch when the wind-storms came in." See JDC, 325; MGED, 37.

225   The original term *Hollander* is taken to mean any subject of the Dutch Republic, not just a person from the province of Holland.

and rule the suburb of Kampung Kling[226] which has been burned down, while the Gentlemen States [General] will have no authority in the matter. If possible, he will take up residence there and have it fortified, and the aforementioned Gentlemen States [General] will assist him with advice in this.

6. After the conquest of the city, His Majesty will have all the guns found in it; he will be able to take away one half of them immediately and undertake to leave the other half in the city for its defense, until guns have been provided by the Gentlemen States [General].

7. That which will be found in the city, merchandise, money, goods and otherwise, will accrue one half to the vassals of the aforementioned Gentlemen States [General] of this fleet and the other half to His Majesty aforementioned.

8. Any merchandise not belonging to the vassals of the aforementioned Gentlemen States [General] will have to be unloaded in the suburb under the authority of the king. The Gentlemen States [General's] vassals will be at liberty to come and buy it and other merchandise there and bring it into the city.

9. Furthermore, they will aid and assist each other with all their might and to their utmost powers to inflict harm upon the Portuguese and the Spanish, their mutual enemies. If any of the parties declare war on another than the Portuguese or the

---

226   A suburb of Melaka that had been reportedly burnt down by the Portuguese when Matelieff had arrived. See CMJ, 549-50.

Spanish, the other party will not be obliged to assist him except in defense only.

10. Neither party will have the power to make peace with the king of Spain without both parties' consent.

11. On both sides, anyone causing a scandal in religious matters will be indicted and punished by the authorities under whom he falls.

12. Should any person of either party have anything to say against another, concerning guilt or otherwise, the defendant will be called before his own authorities.

13. Should one of the Dutch defect to the King of Johor because of any evil crime or otherwise, or from the King's people to the Dutch, parties must undertake to deliver the runaway into the hands of his authorities.

Form of the oath which was sworn to the preceding agreement on both sides.

We, Yang di Pertuan and Raja Seberang, kings of Johor, hereby promise to uphold the agreement written above in all its stipulations and articles, without acting against it in any way. So truly help us God.

I, Cornelis Matelieff de Jonge, in the name of the High Mighty Gentlemen States General of the United Netherlands, hereby promise to adhere to the entire agreement written above in all its parts, without acting against it in any way. So truly help me God....

While drawing up this agreement, the king asked that he be given an abode to be lodged within the city, since most everything had been burned around it; and that the fort be left to satisfy his needs. To this the admiral replied that he wanted to do everything His Majesty asked for, nonetheless requesting the king not to ask for things that would cause him and ours damage in the end. For the governor whom the admiral would appoint had to live in the fort, and making him leave every time His Majesty came would cause him far too many problems. In the end, it was decided that the admiral would provide a house for the king's person where he could stay as often as he wished, accompanied by 15 or 17 persons from his retinue, until such time as a suitable dwelling had been made in Kampung Kling. With this the king was satisfied.

The admiral also conceded all the guns to His Majesty, as well as half the spoils, although earlier he had promised it to his men if they were to take the city by storm, or what else they would negotiate for a ransom. The admiral let the king have the tolls from the foreign nations because he reckoned that all those who came to live in the city would be free, so that many folks would be made to come and populate the city, and over time one would bring in so many people from the fatherland that ours would be powerful enough to defend themselves without Johor, and also to guard all navigation with their own men.

After the conditions had been agreed on (it took a while before they were written down and signed by both kings),[227] our men began to make the tools for landing. But first the admiral handed His Excellency the prince's[228] letter to Raja Seberang, together with the gifts, which were a long

---

227 That is by Ala'udin Ri'ayat Shah III and Raja Bongsu of Johor.

228 That is a reference to Maurice of Nassau, the Stadholder of Holland and Zeeland and titular Prince of Orange.

gun,[229] a double-barreled pistol inlaid with mother of pearl, two more pistols, a riding sword and a partisan,[230] all beautifully made. Then the Gentlemen Directors'[231] gifts as well: a cuirass,[232] two partisans and six shiny cuirasses.[233] In order to prevent jealousy from arising between the brothers, the admiral said to Raja Seberang that he had orders to deliver all the said gifts to the king of Johor,[234] and although [Raja Seberang] had sent his envoys to Holland[235] with presents for His Excellency,[236] it was the Yang di Pertuan who was ruling king. He therefore asked Raja Seberang to explain to him if he would do ill or well by giving him all this. To which Raja Seberang replied that the admiral should rest assured, for his brother would value what he did. With this, the admiral was satisfied....

---

229   A type of pipe shot or barrel gun.

230   A spear-shaped weapon mounted on a pole and used for stabbing. CMJ, 502.

231   The Gentlemen Seventeen.

232   An armor piece for the chest or back, or both.

233   They were probably made of polished steel.

234   King Ala'udin.

235   A reference to the 1603–5 Johor diplomatic mission to the Dutch Republic.

236   The Stadholder, Prince Maurice.

Admiral Matelieff and Tun Sri Lanang

The admiral, realizing that he could not take the city by force nor get help from the Malays,[237] sent his men aboard on 27 May, keeping under arms only 300, as well as 60 or 70 clerks, cooks and the like, with whom he knew he was strong enough to guard his entrenchments. He also had the two half-cannons[238] and iron pieces brought on board, both in order to have less goods ashore if the armada[239] came and to encourage the king to make his people stand guard next to ours. The king, the Yang di Pertuan, was astonished by this, although the admiral had done it after consulting Raja Seberang. He therefore said to the king that his men were tired of guarding all the entrenchments on their own, and fell ill because they could not endure that hot country. [He also said] that they were not pleased at all because they saw the Malays do nothing but go for a walk, not guarding any entrenchment; and [other] similar remarks. The king answered that his people would take better care of the watch from then on. But it was all the same old song, the orang kaya[240] did not want to risk their slaves.

The bendahara [Tun Sri Lanang] even had the audacity to say to the admiral, in the king's presence while he was in his council, that our people had conquered Ternate and Ambon without the inhabitants' help, and therefore they ought to do so in this case as well; for he had not come to fight, but to watch the fight. To which the admiral replied: "I have come here as a servant to the king,[241] the Yang di

---

237   The term here and in subsequent instances is employed to mean the subjects of the Johor ruler.

238   A cannon capable of firing balls of about 12 kilograms.

239   The fleet of the Portuguese viceroy of India.

240   Lit. "rich man"; here a person of influence or good standing. See CMJ, 500.

241   King Ala'udin.

Pertuan, whose war this is.[242] If you do not wish to be his servant, nor do him any service, you can say so; and if the king, Yang di Pertuan, commands me to, I will make such people leave here." When the king heard this, he was annoyed with the bendahara, and many noblemen were very pleased that the admiral spoke to him like that, since he was an arrogant fool and a rude beast, who seemed to be more on the Portuguese than on the Dutch side. His position was that of the king's governor....

Matelieff retreats to the Johor River and surveys Batu Sawar

In the morning of 24 August, our people left for Johor before dawn, following the decision they had made the day before, and on the 25th got out of sight of the Portuguese Armada (which headed for Melaka). On 13 September, they arrived at the Johor River, the king[243] coming out at sea to welcome them to his country. On the 18th of that month, the admiral sailed to Batu Sawar to urge that the king fortify his city; secondly, that he would take measures for the ships to be provided with food; thirdly, to see if there was any gunpowder to be had, of which they had a great shortage; and fourthly, to ask the king to send two perahus to Melaka and one to Aceh, to see if four Dutch ships had arrived there, as was being said—which at that point would have been a big thing for our state in the East Indies. At this request, the king sent one perahu to Melaka instead of the two that he was asked for. The perahu to Aceh was not to follow. Gunpowder

---

242 This could be taken as specific evidence that the purpose of the Johor diplomatic mission to the Dutch Republic in 1603–5 involved an invitation extended by Johor to the Dutch to assist them in a military campaign against Portuguese Melaka.

243 King Ala'udin.

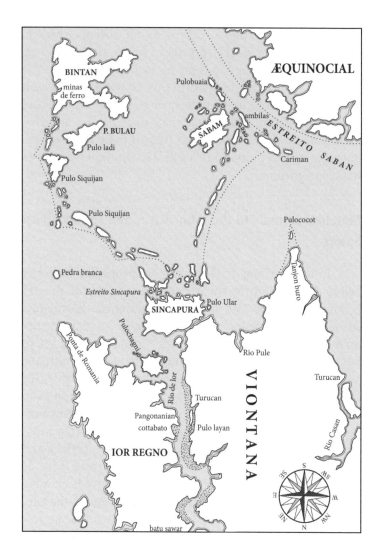

Hand-drawn map of Singapore and the Johor River to Batu Sawar by Manuel Godinho de Erédia (redrawn by Ms. Lee Li Kheng, GIS and Map Resource Unit, National University of Singapore). The original is found in Erédia's Declaraçam de Malaca (Description of Melaka), c.1613, fol. 45 recto.

was not to be had, but for about 10 *taels*,[244] and it cost 4 *emas*[245] for 10 *gantang*;[246] and it was finely ground powder besides, which is not much good. It would have been possible to erect a powder mill, and at low cost as well, because there is wood and water running down in abundance there and one can get both saltpeter and sulphur enough—the only thing is that there are no people to organize and produce it.

The admiral surveyed the city with his captains. It was well suitable for fortification against any Portuguese attack, but the Malays do not want to work. He drew a plan as to how they should fortify the city and they promised to follow it, but as soon as he had returned to the ships they refused to work. In short: if the Dutch had wanted to come and fortify Batu Sawar themselves, that would not have been a bad thing as far as the Malays were concerned. As to getting a perahu to send to Aceh, it was the same old song: they expected one from Banten, but it never turned up. The king had given his people orders for the victuals, but nothing arrived at the ships. Arak could not be bought at any price, and their wine had almost run out. Then the admiral went to the ships and immediately sent his vice-admiral to Batu Sawar to ask the king's opinion and make a decision after that. There were a lot of problems tormenting him. For if they left for Banten or Ambon, it was to be feared that the Portuguese would come and lay siege to Batu Sawar right away, and no doubt conquer it as well. Doing battle against the fleet again was dangerous with so little gunpowder and cannon-balls and there was no powder to be had except in Aceh, which was far away, and time would run out to send the *Amsterdam* and the *Witte Leeuw*[247] to Banten and from there to the fatherland. Leaving

---

244 About 380 grams. See CMJ, 518; JDC, 345.

245 Equivalent to about 15 grams of mint-grade gold. See CMJ, 473; JDC, 318-9.

246 Equivalent to a volume of about 17.5 liters. See CMJ, 479.

247 Two ships from Matelieff's fleet. See CMJ, 188n249.

the fleet alone completely and going away like that was detrimental to all the neighboring kings, who would suffer a lot. Our people, moreover, might even be chased from that region altogether, which they need so much for the trade with China.

Description of Johor's capital Batu Sawar and of the nearby settlement Kota Seberang

The city of Batu Sawar lies on the Johor River, about five or six [Dutch nautical] miles[248] from the sea.[249] It is a very beautiful river, broad and deep, subject to ebb and flood up to the city, but before the city it is fresh.[250] Most of the land is lowland. The people mostly live along the river. The houses are built on poles. There are two places which are called fortress; one of them is Batu Sawar, the other lies on the opposite side of the river and is called Kota Seberang. Batu Sawar is about 1,300 *treden*[251] in circumference, built as a square with high palisades 40 feet[252] tall and linked closely together; it has some fortifications to the side, but not well made. It lies on a flat field close to the river. The nearest hills are a quarter of a mile[253] away from it. One could easily make the river[254] surround it. Inside, the city is closely packed with straw[255] houses, apart from those belonging to the king and some

---

248 About 44.5 kilometers. See CMJ, 496-7.
249 Another translation of this passage can be found in GPFT, appendix 11, 207–9.
250 Although tidal conditions from the sea still condition the flow of the Johor River, the water at Batu Sawar is fresh and not saline.
251 About 1 kilometer.
252 About 11.2 meters.
253 About 1 kilometer.
254 The Johor River.
255 Here almost certainly *atap* houses.

noblemen, which are made of wood. In Batu Sawar and Kota Seberang combined, it is estimated that there are no less than 3,000 to 4,000 fighting men, but most of the people live outside the fortress. If there is an emergency, they all burn down their houses and go to the fortress, for they can make a new house quickly, each with his slaves. All the land belongs to the king and is hardly valued, so that whoever asks it of him can receive enough land. It appears to be very fertile nonetheless, for it is full of trees and the grass reaches a man's belly. But the land is not cultivated, for if they turned to agriculture they would have everything in abundance, whereas now they are in want of many things. The king often gave the admiral presents in the form of refreshments. One time he gave him, among other things, three sugar canes 18 feet long and 7 inches thick.[256] The admiral had never heard of such a thing and was quite astonished. Kota Seberang may be some 400 or 500 *treden* in circumference and is square as well.[257] Not many people live there, and the riverside where they live is also defended by palisades. The land lies low and is flooded with every spring tide, so that one cannot bring cannons into position outside the city. The admiral told them to make three bulwarks to begin with to flank the walls—the idea pleased them, but they were afraid of the work....

Negotiations for the second Johor-Dutch Treaty, September, 1606

... Three or four days later, Raja Seberang came down again with the bendahara[258] (which means something like "governor"). They had deliberated a long time in Batu Sawar upon the admiral's request that, because the contract signed before

---

256 About 5 meters by 18 centimeters.

257 About 300-375 meters.

258 Tun Sri Lanang

Melaka could not be made effective as to the ownership of the city for the Gentlemen States [General] and that of the country for the king, the king would therefore grant ours such and so big a place as the admiral wished, be it on any of the islands such as Lingga, Bintan or Karimun[259] or on the mainland at the Johor River, wherever a suitable place was found, in order to build dwellings, warehouses, armories, shipyards and otherwise. Then families would be brought there from Holland, so that one would have all kinds of crafts and business there. His Majesty's lands would profit from this and could then be provided with everything necessary. All other articles would remain in effect, and it would last until the Lord God would grant us a better basis for an attack on Melaka.... [260]

{Second agreement between the two said parties, made in the city of Batu Sawar on 23 September, 1606.

Firstly, all the articles included in the agreement made between the parties on the ship *Oranje* at the roadstead of Melaka on 17 May of this year are confirmed.

But since it has not pleased the Lord God Almighty to let us conquer the city and fortress of Melaka thus far, so that some articles on both sides cannot be kept, namely owning the city for the Gentlemen

---

259 These three names refer to islands in the Riau Archipelago (now in Indonesia). The islands are located to the south and in the case of Karimun to the west of the Singapore Straits.

260 The following section marked in brackets representing the text of the second Dutch-Johor treaty of 1606 has been moved from the original position in the text where it had been wrongly placed, and inserted here. For the original location see CMJ, 159-60.

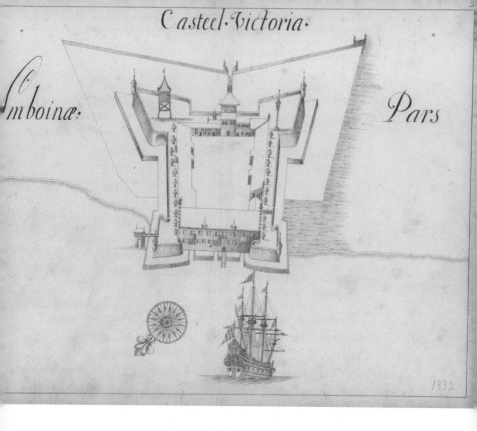

Undated bird's-eye view of Fort Victoria on Ambon. The Hague: National Archives of the Netherlands: 4.VEL 1332.

States [General], and owning the suburb as well as all the land for the King of Johor, we wish to postpone this to a later occasion, when it will please God to grant us the favor of conquering it by the industry of the Gentlemen States [General] and the King of Johor.

Since it is necessary for the Gentlemen States [General] to have a secure and permanent place for their subjects to further their trade in the East Indies, to gather and keep their goods, merchandise, ammunition, gear and otherwise, and if necessary to bring craftsmen and families from their country: His Majesty the King of Johor will give

111

to the Gentlemen States [General] or their captain such a place as they will desire, either here on the mainland or on any island under His Majesty's authority, as big or small as the Gentlemen States or their captain will see fit, to build their houses and dwellings there and own them as they would Melaka.

On the other hand, the Gentlemen States and their subjects undertake to uphold the articles included in the agreement made before Melaka. Thus done at Batu Sawar on the date as above....}

... They took the opportunity to bring forward a few things they requested from the admiral. Firstly, that he would take it upon himself to give the king a loan if he needed it, of 300 or 400 to no less than 1,000 reals-of-eight.[261] The king was to pay it back in such goods as the factor[262] asked for, and the king was not to ask for another loan before the first one had been [fully] repaid. Secondly: that the Gentlemen States [General] would help him with all their might against all his enemies without any exceptions, both offensively and defensively. Thirdly: that said Gentlemen States at his request would assist him with men from the ships, guns, ammunition and whatever else he needed; indeed that if any of their ships were in the vicinity of Johor, he could summon them to his service. They further wanted the admiral to stay moored there with the ships until others arrived from Holland, for as long as the Dutch were moored there the people of Batu

---

261 The reference is here to silver coin minted in the Spanish Americas with a face value of 8 reals and containing a little over 27 grams of silver. See CJM, 510-11; JDC, 338-9. The sums indicated are thus equivalent to about 8.1, 10.8 and 27 kilograms of coin-grade silver respectively.

262 This is a reference to the head of the VOC factory at Batu Sawar. See the glossary (*factor, factory*).

Sawar and the king did not fear. But as soon as they left, the king thought that the Portuguese would arrive immediate- ly,[263] and he and his people would be lost. As Raja Seberang said to the admiral in secret: the noblemen and citizens of Batu Sawar were mostly inclined to run away up the river and had told him that if he wanted to fight the Portuguese, he could do it with the Dutch, and so on. If he was granted this request, he wanted to give our people a location of 30 fathoms, that is 120 square fathoms.[264]

The admiral answered Raja Seberang and the benda- hara that the Gentlemen States [General] were not the kind of people for whom one had to lay down an amount of 500 or 1,000 reals-of-eight[265] in a treaty in their name. But if the Dutch conducted their trade in his country, as they hoped, there would be days when he would make a profit of 1,000 reals-of-eight. Therefore the admiral did not wish to include it in the agreement, but (although he was only a private indi- vidual) he wanted to give the king 1,000 reals-of-eight as a gift from his own money, if he stayed a friend of the Dutch, and spend it for him in Holland on guns, swords and what- ever else he might want. He was therefore surprised that the king thought so little of the alliance with the Dutch; for if he had no hope of more advantage from it than he showed on

---

263   The Portuguese imposed blockades on the Johor River when the Dutch ships were not at anchor. In some cases, they launched military campaigns against the upstream towns as André Furtado de Mendonça did in 1603 and again in 1604. The Dutch had also stepped up violence against the Portuguese between 1603 and 1605. See SMS, 88–101.

264   The fathom is a unit to measure the depth of water. From the subsequent text it appears that the plot of land in question measured about 30 by 40 Dutch fathoms, that is about 50.7 by 67.6 meters; a total plot size of about 3,427 square meters. See also CMJ, 523.

265   These sums are equivalent to between 13.5 and 27 kilograms of coin-grade silver.

the exterior, then it would not be advisable for him to resist the Portuguese with ours. That was where this first point came to a halt, and the Malays did not speak of it again.

The admiral replied to the second point that the Gentlemen States [General] were not inclined to wage an unjust war against anyone, nor to risk their subjects for an evil or unknown cause. Accordingly they were prepared to take on defensive war for him, but not offensive war; unless it was against the Portuguese, whom they had already declared to be their enemies. Raja Seberang then asked if they would help him if the king of Banten,[266] where our people have their house and factory, came to make war upon him. The admiral answered that they would willingly help him against all and everyone, as much as was in their power, if anyone came to fight him. Turning friends into enemies for someone else's sake, however, was not something the Gentlemen States [General] intended to do, unless they had been informed of the situation beforehand. With this answer they let themselves be contented, finding it just and fair.

It was unnecessary to respond to the third point, for when our people were there with their ships, they would always do their best in his defense; and then they could employ their people and guns in his service better than the Malays might, and His Majesty would be better served by them than otherwise. They[267] were of the same opinion.

The admiral was surprised that the king presented him with a place 30 fathoms long:[268] if our people were to have their shipyard there, they would need a place at least six times bigger to equip their ships. Thus he did not want 30 fathoms, but as much as he would need, without limit; for the bigger the place, the bigger the trade would be, apart from the fact that land is not worth anything there and is

---

266   Pangeran Ratu.

267   Raja Seberang and Tun Sri Lanang.

268   Just under 51 meters.

not considered valuable. The admiral almost suspected that the reason they proposed a limit to him was that they think our people are like the Portuguese, who start by asking for a place to build a house, then it becomes a fort, and in the end they enslave the people. He therefore said to him that the king ought to question the ambassadors who had been to Holland thoroughly about the country's government there. Then he would find that it did not permit the incorporation of anybody's land, but only trade. Indeed he assured him that if His Majesty wished to have the island of Ambon, which our people had taken from the Portuguese,[269] the Gentlemen States [General] would no doubt put it at his disposal, as long as they were certain that he would keep it well and let nobody do business there but ours, who cared only for trade and not for land. Raja Seberang answered that he trusted our nation completely, and did not harbor such suspicions against it. He had taken it that our people wanted their location within the fortress of Batu Sawar, where there was little space, and most of it inhabited by the nobility and others. But if the admiral wanted land outside the fortress, the king would give him as much as he needed. This was just an excuse because they were disappointed in their demand, but one should assume they mean well and rely on them and their power in as far as one can use it to one's advantage.

Consequently the treaty remained unsigned at that point, but orally he promised to give our people as much land as they would need, in any place they themselves would ask for. To his request that the admiral remain moored there until other ships from Holland arrived, the answer was given that this was not well feasible, for two ships had to leave for Holland in December or else wait for a whole year—and then they would be unable, their provisions consumed and their sails, ropes and the rest worn down. But the admiral would

---

269   Steven van der Hagen had taken Ambon for the Dutch in 1605.
       See also the list of place names (*Ambon*).

be able to stay near Melaka until December, and during that time the Portuguese would not venture there.[270] This pleased Raja Seberang who said that he would announce it to his brother [King Ala'udin] and went back to the city. At this time there were 1,034 mouths to feed left on the fleet.

In the evening of 6 October, the admiral went to Batu Sawar, where he spoke with Raja Seberang about signing the second contract.[271] Raja Seberang had refused the vice-admiral this earlier because he wanted some extra conditions (as explained above). The admiral admonished him: if they did not want to keep the contract made before Melaka,[272] they only had to say so, for he allowed them their liberty. If they did not want to resume the matter of Melaka, then he would do it alone now, since he saw enough possibilities—or if he could not do it alone, he would get the help of the neighboring kings (the kings of Aceh, Kedah,[273] Siam or Pegu,[274] for instance) and make an alliance with them. He added that the Gentlemen States [General] would never make a peace with the Portuguese without including all their allies in it.[275] Raja

---

270   In fact, Matelieff's ships remained in the Melaka and Singapore Straits region until early January 1607. He was wrong, however, about the Portuguese.

271   This evidently refers to the contract of 23 September, 1606, which had not yet been signed and sworn.

272   This refers to the contract of 17 May, 1606.

273   River, port, settlement and polity in the northwestern regions of the Malay Peninsula, important in the context of the pepper and tin trade. In the 16th and 17th centuries, the Portuguese regarded Kedah as a vassal or client state of Siam. It was attacked and overrun by Aceh in 1619.

274   In earlier centuries, Pegu was home to a Mon kingdom. In this period the city served as the capital of a kingdom ruled by the Taungoo dynasty ("Burma") until 1635. See CMJ, 569, 582; CMJ, 374, 382-3.

275   This indeed came to pass at the time of signing the Twelve Years' Truce with the Spanish Empire in April 1609, when the

Seberang replied that they valued the contract made before Melaka and wished to adhere to it. Then the admiral went to King [Ala'udin], who avowed all that his brother[276] had dealt with, had the second contract drawn up, and signed it. He also said that if the admiral (in accordance with his promise) actually ensured that the Portuguese did not come there for two months, he would be able to fortify his city sufficiently in the meantime; for his people could arrive any day now from all the surrounding islands to work on the fortification.

A similar inclination and resolve was displayed by several persons from the nobility, such as the Raja Dili,[277] Sri [Raja] Mahkota,[278] Raja Lela,[279] the temenggong or admiral (an intelligent man), and Sri Amar di Raja,[280] who asked the admiral to put it to the king in earnest and insist strongly, even threaten him that the admiral would leave at once if he did not fortify his city—as they themselves would. But they were afraid to arouse his displeasure because he was a man who became very difficult if one addressed him about matters of state, but who could drink and party for eight days on end without tiring. Hence Sri Amar di Raja candidly told the admiral when they were alone that if he wanted to send the Dutch to work on the fortress, that would be a great service to the king. But the admiral replied that that would be completely unreasonable and a great shame for all the world,

---

Land's Advocate Johan van Oldenbarnevelt ensured that the Asian allies of the Dutch Republic were included in the truce arrangements, and especially the explanation of article 4 of the truce agreement ratified by the French and English in the Treaty of Guarantee on 17 June 1609. See GPFT, 70, 310–1 notes 142–3.

276 King Ala'udin.

277 The ruler of a kingdom in north-central Sumatra. See the list of place names *(Aru)*.

278 See the glossary *(Raja Mahkota)*.

279 See the glossary *(Raja Lela)*.

280 See the glossary *(Amar di Raja)*.

that warriors who know how to handle a gun and never turn their back to the enemy would labor while slaves who were unworthy to be likened to the least of his people would stand by and watch, especially since it would be for the protection of the slaves' own land. The king himself would not want to use such men as the Dutch, who came to his service; but that they were willing to do anything. Thus Sri Amar di Raja was put to shame and said that he had only made a joke, and the admiral should take it as such. The nobility did not seem at all inclined to make peace with the Portuguese, as the admiral in particular had sufficiently explained to them the untrustworthiness of the Portuguese, who had no other intention than deceiving them and separating the Dutch from them in order to deal with them as they wished. This the Johorese understood well.

On the 7th of that month, the admiral went to the king to take his leave. While he was waiting for an opportunity to talk to him, Raja Seberang told him that seven or eight prisoners from Melaka had been brought to Muar.[281] They declared that the Portuguese were going to ask the Johorese for peace and would make every effort for it. For the man who was coming as the new governor of Melaka,[282] Dom António de Meneses, son of Dom Duarte de Meneses, the former viceroy of the Indies,[283] had declared that if the present viceroy[284] did not make peace with the king of Johor, he had no wish to accept the governorship of Melaka. Raja

---

281 The region around Muar was at the time under the control of Johor. It had its own shahbandar and was ruled by Raja Gila. See CMJ, 563.

282 André Furtado de Mendonça served a three-year term from the middle of the calendar year 1603 to 1606.

283 Duarte de Meneses (also spelled Menezes) served as viceroy between 1584 and 1588. His son António, the Lord of Sardoal, served as captain (governor) of Portuguese Melaka between 1606 and 1607.

284 Martim Alfonso de Castro.

Seberang asked the admiral to ask the king for his opinion on the matter; for if he was inclined to peace, Raja Seberang had decided to leave with the Dutch and go to the island of Lingga, which he hoped to defend against the Portuguese with the help of the Dutch. But when the admiral came to the king, he found him so favorably inclined toward him that he did not think it necessary to discuss the matter at length with him, but he did discuss the aforementioned prisoners and the decision of the Portuguese. The king answered that he did not want peace with the Portuguese, because he found no reliability in them, only deceit.

On 9 October, the admiral went on board. The king came to visit him on the 11th, saying that he had news of two Portuguese ships, three galleys and several foists waiting at Pulau Karimun to escort the junks coming to Melaka from Makassar[285] and Java with merchandise and food. Seven more ships had gone north, either to return to Aceh or to escort the ship from the Coromandel [Coast][286] or São Tomé.[287] Because of this news, all our men thought it advisable to leave immediately and then see what was to be done next. The galley was therefore equipped to go to Ambon with 20 or 25 soldiers, 15 or 20 sailors and 40 blacks[288] they

285 Name of a port (between 1971 to 1999 known as Ujung Pandang) and polity in the south of the great island of Sulawesi (Celebes). Makassar was important in the context of the seaborn trade and also the bulk trade in spices (cloves and nutmeg from the Malukus) and rice.

286 The southeastern coast of subcontinental India, approximately equivalent to the coastal regions of Tamil Nadu State.

287 São Tomé de Meliapore is situated on the Coromandel Coast in the present-day Indian state of Tamil Nadu close to Chennai (Madras). In 1522, the Portuguese discovered what they believed was the grave of Thomas the Apostle. This city is commonly known by two different names: São Tomé or Mylapur.

288 This is a Dutch expression commonly employed to refer to persons of color generally. Here it generically refers to a Southeast

still had left after getting them at Melaka. It was also decided to go to Melaka via Singapore[289] with the ships, in order to attack the enemy, if an opportunity presented itself.

Asian local of indistinct origin. The term was used here and in subsequent instances as a pejorative, but not exclusively so, so caution is advised.

289   Read here: via the Singapore Straits.

Document 2

Excerpt from Matelieff's memorial
of June, 1607
Entitled
Discourse on the State
and Trade of the Indies

[This short exposé has not hitherto been counted among the memorials of Matelieff. This is because a manuscript copy does not survive, but the memorial was published by Isaac Commelin within the running text of the *Historische Verhael*, or *Journal*, of Matelieff's voyage. The range of subjects covered in this document overlap with other memorials and include the advantages and disadvantages that the Portuguese and Spanish have over the Dutch in the East Indies, as well as trading opportunities in certain commodities and at certain ports around Asia. Significantly, Matelieff staked out the different branches of intra-Asian trade and intimated that a monopolization of the nutmeg trade should be pursued as a genuine possibility. For pepper, however, he suggested a completely different strategy: ruin the margins and drive the European competitors out of business by carrying pepper as ships' ballast and dumping the product on the European market. This document is important for the history of the Singapore-Johor nexus as it identifies Johor as one of the principal marketplaces for pepper in Southeast Asia.]

Surveying the state of our fatherland—where we are troubled by so great a war within the country, dealing with so powerful an enemy as Albert of Austria,[289] who is supported by the House of Spain and his own House of Austria[290]—I believe that we will not be able to sustain the cause of the East Indies by letting it be governed by the Gentlemen Directors alone. I do not see that they will gain sufficient authority here in the [East] Indies to bring the matter to a good end, since we are dealing with the Spanish and Portuguese, who started here over a century ago and have taken root very firmly in the country, having many strongholds, a multitude of people and an established government, so that they can carry out all their business from a firmer ground than we can. We have to bring people from Holland, half exhausted from the long journey, whereas they get them all fresh from their territories nearby. For although here in the Portuguese Indies they do not have enough people to manage their business and protect themselves from our nation's fleets, they nonetheless find it much easier to bring in people than we do, because the ships coming from Portugal only have to put the men ashore at Goa. From there, their armadas are equipped which then are fresh again, just like the Spaniards coming from Manila.[291]

If we want to do anything useful here in the Indies, therefore, we have to see to it that we obtain a place[292] as well, where we can rest when we come from Holland. This will

---

289   Albert VII, Archduke of Austria had married Princess Isabella, who had been given the Southern and Northern Low Countries as her dowry by her father King Philip II of Spain.

290   The Houses of Spain and Austria were members of the Habsburg family.

291   This toponym could also be read from the Philippines in general. See CMJ, 557-8.

292   A rendezvous or permanent base.

bring us much profit, such as the restoration of our people and ships in the first place, and secondly the increase of our reputation with the Indian princes and peoples who thus far do not place much trust in us, saying: "It's true that the Dutch are good people, better than Spanish and Portuguese, but what use is it? They come here in passing only, and once they have their ships full they leave again. Without help, we are unable to defend ourselves against the Spanish and the Portuguese who come and ruin us once the Dutch are gone because we have traded with the Dutch. The Spanish and Portuguese on the other hand protect us, and the Dutch (although they could overpower us) do not harm us even though we trade with the Spanish and Portuguese. It is therefore better for us to stay friends with the Portuguese: in that way, we are not destroyed completely.

These must be their deliberations, and moreover the Portuguese are doing their utmost to make it clear to the Indians that we do not have any power, but are just a disorganized people because we do not choose a permanent residence here in the Indies as they do. So we have to obtain one, or all our business is worth nothing.

The entire trade in the East Indies consists in the following parts:

1. Pepper,[293] to be obtained at Banten, Johor, Patani, Kedah and Aceh.
2. Cloves,[294] to be obtained at Ambon and the Malukus.
3. Nutmeg and mace,[295] to be obtained at Banda.[296]

---

293 See the glossary (*pepper*).
294 See the glossary (*clove*).
295 See the glossary (*mace, nutmeg*).
296 Island group located to the south of the Malukus. The Bandas, including its main island Lontor (Great Banda), was renowned

4. The Cambay[297] trade.
5. The Coromandel[298] trade with pieces of cloth, and the Bengal[299] trade, unknown so far.
6. The China trade, and attached to it, Japan.

If these goods are not all in one party's hands, either those of the Portuguese or ours, we will ruin each other and give the goods a high price here in the Indies but a low price in Europe.

Now as regards to pepper: it is not well feasible for us to get it into our hands alone, for apart from the Portuguese, the English[300] sail to Banten as well, and they also have their house and factory there. The English are trading completely at ease while we wage war against the Portuguese, so that both they and the people of Banten are protected by us without having to bear any costs. It is not feasible either to make the king of Banten, who is still a child, make a solid decision to trade with us alone, or it would have to cost big money. Indeed, that would still achieve nothing, for I am convinced that he and all other Indian princes, no matter how strong a treaty they had made with us or anybody else, will break it as soon as they are in a bit of trouble or can make a better profit. Therefore we should not aim for that, but try to make sure that the English do not obtain any other spices besides pepper, and that we bring pepper over as well, as ballast, put-

---

for the cultivation of nutmeg and its by-product mace. Banda was taken by the Dutch in 1609.

297   Principal port city on the western coast of India at Gujarat. See also the list of place names (*Cambay*).

298   The southeastern coast of India.

299   Kingdom located at the northern shore of the Bay of Bengal and now largely divided between India and Bangladesh. Bengal was conquered by the Moghuls in 1576 who governed the province (via the Nawab of Bengal) with varying degrees of self-administration and control.

300   That means ships of the Honorable East India Company (EIC).

ting such a price on it that they cannot make a profit on it, and that the other goods alone can give us our profit.

Getting all the nutmeg and mace into our hands is, in my view, something that can be achieved.[301] To avoid having to take the island of Banda and build a fortress there (which, apart from the cost which is high, would give us a bad name with the Indian princes), one should take the matter in hand as follows.

The king of Makassar[302] is a ruler mighty in people who has a country rich in rice and all kinds of foodstuffs, so that Melaka's food mostly comes from his country; the same is true of Banda, where he sends rice every year. I would make an agreement with him and send three ships which would put ashore 200 men (combined with the Makassarese, that would be enough for Banda), with a promise to help him take the land and to surrender it to him without claiming anything of it for ourselves. But on the condition that no one be allowed to come and take in cargo there but we, and that we purchase the mace and nutmeg from him at a certain price, namely the one current at this moment. I do not doubt that he would enter upon such an agreement, and then one could further stipulate that he build a house for us there at his expense, as big and strong as we wish, to keep our wares in it and to be secure from any attacks by enemies. We could then have it built at any location and as well-positioned as we liked, and since the king would not be present there, with presents we could have the orang kaya[303] build whatever we wanted. As a consequence, a great enemy would have arisen for the Portuguese, and a great friend to us. One could make other conditions with him as well to secure the land, for

---

301   Matelieff is suggesting the creation of a monopoly here.

302   King Ala'udin, the first Muslim ruler of Gowa. Makassar was a major trading city located in the south of the island of Celebes (present-day Sulawesi).

303   Notables; persons of status. See also the glossary (*orang kaya*).

example, he would take all Banda's nobility into his country and give them a place to live there, while bringing some of his own noblemen to Banda. That all the nobility would live in just one place on Banda, and that instead of the four or five cities there are now, a single city would be made, where we would have our house. That they—the people living in the country, that is—would be obliged to come to the market there every fortnight and deliver their goods to the factory. That as soon as the produce was harvested and treated, they would deliver them to the merchant and be paid immediately as well. And to avoid the disorder of the great debts the Bandanese tend to incur, and which they cannot pay afterward: that it would be forbidden to issue loans to each other, at a certain penalty. I believe that in this way, we would have Banda in our grip, and the king of Makassar bound to us in the best way.

But getting the cloves into our hands alone is difficult to achieve. Of the cloves from Ambon, Luhu[304] and Kambelo[305] we have sufficient quantity, but we lack those from the Malukus, which cannot be remedied unless we drive the Spaniards from Ternate. If that would be easy to achieve I leave to anyone's judgment, but I will not refrain from writing down my opinion on the matter. I think it can be done, if we start from a sound basis and attack Melaka once more. For if the Portuguese lose Melaka, they would be unable to assist the Malukus from Goa. And in my opinion, one could at a low cost prevent the Spanish from supplying Ternate with victuals from Manila. One should start by visiting the king of Mindanao[306] with three or four ships. He

---

304 A city on the island of Hoamoal peninsula located on the western side of the main island of Seram. In the early 17th century, the population of Luhu was loyal to the ruler of Ternate.

305 A city on Hoamoal. At the dawn of the 17th century, the people of Kambelo were loyal to the ruler of Ternate.

306 Island in the present-day Philippines.

is powerful in people and it is said that he can equip no less than 50 kora-kora,[307] with which one could go to the island Panama or Panay,[308] which lies near Manila. There is a place called Oton[309] there, where there are 18 Spanish soldiers, with a number of other Spanish inhabitants so that there may be 40 whites in all. That place I would take and destroy—or if the blacks of Mindanao wanted to keep it, they would be welcome to it—for it is rich in rice and all other foodstuffs, which are taken from there to Ternate. From there, I would go to Manila and destroy all the ships I found there so that they could not help Ternate. After that, I would send a ship of 80 or 100 lasts back to Mindanao to remain in the Tagima Strait,[310] with the kora-kora from Mindanao, to catch those who still wanted to reach Ternate (for they would have no other way); so that after one had done this once or twice, there would be great famine at Ternate. For as regards bombarding and damaging Ternate, I believe that the Spaniards will now reinforce it and put so many men there that it would take a big force. He will find it difficult to provide the Malukus with cloth, for the little bit that he now takes there is brought to him at Manila by the Chinese. This will also make the Ternatans unhappy over time, if they are not pro-

---

307   An oared war ship commonly used in the Malukus, especially in Ambon. A kora-kora can carry between 50 and 70 men, and some large royal kora-kora can carry up to 300 oarsmen and warriors.

308   The name Panama for the island of Panay features notably in the maps of the late 16th and early 17th century by Dutch cartographers Cornelis Claesz. and Pieter Plancius. The name Panati in Matelieff's original evidently represents a corruption of the toponym Panay.

309   Oton is a port located on the southern coast of the island Panay in the Philippines.

310   Tagima was the former name of Basilan Island in the Philippines. The strait in question runs between the islands Basilan (south) and Mindanao (north).

vided with cloth, which must be done from Melaka. If one could bring a galley to Ternate, that would seriously harm the Spanish as well.

The China trade also depends on Melaka, for if we controlled that, the Portuguese could no longer sail there. As regards China itself, I do not know enough to write about that yet; once I have been there, I will be able to do it in a better-founded way.

The Coromandel trade with the pieces of cloth, whereby all of the East Indies where we sail now is supplied, is of greater importance; for these countries must have those pieces of cloth, no matter what they cost, but each has its special type which is made in its special place, so that Nagapattinam[311] does not produce what Masulipatam[312] produces. And if the Portuguese lost Melaka, they would have neither the means nor the opportunity to sell their pieces of cloth easily, even if they still had Nagapattinam. But if no way can be found to lay siege to Melaka once more, the Portuguese will seek a way to keep us from the Coromandel trade with their foists; for since it is a level coast overall, they can easily stay between the land and our ships. Also, the ships sailing there are not safe, if the Portuguese want to make an effort. They can deliver a message to Goa over land in eight days and then equip ships against us there. It is also certain that if the Portuguese lost Melaka, they would have to give up the Coromandel Coast, for they would have nowhere to go with the pieces of cloth and thus the coast would not make up for their expenses. In my opinion, there-

---

311   A port located on the Coromandel Coast and effectively controlled by the Portuguese. In the early 17th century, it exported cotton pieces to Southeast Asia. See JDC, 371.

312   Port on the southeastern (Coromandel) coast of India. Masulipatam maintained close trading connections in textiles with Bengal and was known for its cloth pieces and finished clothing. See JDC, 370.

Overleaf: Hand-drawn ground plan of the city of Nagapattinam on the Coromandel Coast of India. The Hague: National Archives of the Netherlands 4.VEL 1082.

fore, the East Indies trade depends mostly on Melaka.

The king of Banten could be brought to see reason as well, if he saw that we had a permanent residence, and that the English, having no access to anything but pepper, had no big trade there. All the pepper coming to Banten from Jambi, Indragiri[313] and other places would [then] come to Melaka, where they would find a better supply of pieces of cloth than at Banten.

In Bengal I do not know that the Portuguese have any power. All the people I have heard speak of the place say that one would find good trade there. There are two ports, one called Porto Pequeno,[314] the other Porto Grande.[315] As I remember, Porto Grande is the most westerly, falling under the king of Cambay,[316] and there is nothing special to be had there but rice, which is brought from there to Cochin[317] in great quantity. Porto Pequeno lies more to the east, and

---

313   River, port and polity located in central-eastern Sumatra. Indragiri was an important port in the early modern pepper trade. See JDC, 351.

314   Sircar has identified Porto Pequeno with Hughli or specifically Satgaon. See D.C. Sircar, *Studies in the Geography of Ancient and Medieval India* (Delhi: Shanti Lal Jain, 1971), 136.

315   Sircar claims that Porto Grande corresponded to a Portuguese settlement in the city of Chittagong in Bengal (now Bangladesh). As Sircar and Moreland have already underscored, however, the Portuguese term *porto* can have a more flexible meaning and also refer to a broader estuary region. See Sircar, *Studies*, 136.

316   This is a reference to the sultan of Gujarat.

317   Port located along the southwestern or Malabar Coast. It remained under Portuguese rule from 1503 to 1663, after which Cochin was ceded to the VOC. See JDC, 358.

A M

Bolwerken en vastigheden
om de Stadt

A. De Punt Amsterdam
B. Watervest
C. Vryney
D. Alckmaer
E. Zeeburg
F. Woerden
G. Leyden
H. 't Watervest
I. De Punt Vrieburgson
K. Ditto ...... Hoorn
L. Ditto ... Delft
M. Ditto ... Rotterdam
N. Ditto ... Middelburgh

De voorstad, genaamt
Hoormandelan

1 Den Bargh
2 Oranjien
3
4 Wyck te dine Soede
5
6 Toemerant
7
8 Groeningen
9 Gelderia
10 Zeelandia
11 Hollandia
12 De Hooftwacht
13 Toegende wachten
14 De Raetsplaats
15 Blaauwesaurwy
16 De Bassia
17 Popehoed
18 Totheyson
19 't Groote Theephuys
20 Bleechery
21 Christingen
22 De Nolybassia
23 De Poort Oranjien
24 De Poort Zelandia

Sentysche Pagoden

25 Nedenanheil
26 Animanda Rajenheil
27 Elemenheil
28 Monimanheil
29 Pagoda Touliaaneil
30 Cottam Cliam, ofte Sarapunenenn
31 Wasspatrananeil
32 Watermananeneil
33 Allaginaheil
34 Animanda Rajenheil
35 Tyzimalheil
36 Sefimanheil
37 Angalamenheil
38 Chembile Touliaanheil
39 Cajagagopoulaaneil
40 Allagifonia Touliaaneil
41 Sollirpoulean
41½ Nagaleona
42 Amkipoulaaneil
43 Sindatisay Touliaaneil
44 Catnigronil
44½ Maleieanomundeil
45 Nagmadanheil
45½ Remandanheil
46 Emmindanheil
47 Ceemmanadanheil ofte Pagode de Zee
48 Wyfienanhdeil
49 Kagasagapoterienheil
50 Indamjanandeil

Moorsche Tempels

58 Pidipalley
59 Ceatimanadapalley
60 Miaspalley
61 De Pagode China
62 Walstimayponliaaneil
63 De Bromin de Thaye van de Pagod China
64 De Siet Comonlaay, hier is goet Drinckwater
65 welspringt van de Rivier
66 Bargh over dese Springs
67 Sanden

Moorsche Tempels

51 Ammanande Sicaaneil
52 Anathaysponliaaneil
53 Poriendeipoulienpheil
54 Caledanadgadeil
55 Catraspordeil
56 Crimanadeil
57 Liecafstimandam, steen is te Miine

Right: Hand-drawn map of the Palembang (left) and Jambi (right) Rivers with their upstream settlements dating from the 17th century. The Hague: National Archives of the Netherlands 4.VEL 364.

much cloth is to be had there. Then we should try trading at Arakan[318] with a few ships. The king[319] much invites us; there is a Portuguese, Felipe de Brito,[320] who has a fortress there, occupied by about 80 Portuguese, lying as many as 50 miles inland,[321] with which he keeps the whole game there muddled so that the king of Arakan, although mighty in people, cannot find a way to drive him out of there. The same Portuguese by these means keeps the whole land of Pegu, which has now been ruined by civil war, in a state of turmoil, and he owns great riches and many [gem]stones.

At Cambay in my view, nothing can be done at this point as long as the Portuguese are so strong on the Malabar Coast[322] and the king there does not yet favor us more. They have to know us better and expose themselves more to the Portuguese, for as long as the king of Cambay does not want to free his rivers, so that we may go freely there, it will all be a perilous business. No large ships are allowed to enter there, and it is so near Goa that if the Portuguese were to hear that

---

318   An early modern coastal kingdom at the Bay of Bengal in what is now approximately the Rakhine State of Myanmar. Its former capital is now known as Mrauk-U. The kingdom remained independent until 1784. See CMJ, 520.

319   A reference to Min Razagri, King of Arakan.

320   Reference is here to Syriam, a fortress held by the Portuguese adventurer Filipe de Brito de Nicote and his men.

321   About 195 kilometers.

322   The coast of southwestern India facing the Arabian Sea, stretching from Cape Comorin (marking the southernmost point of the continental mainland) to the Kerala coast in the north. This broadly covers the coastal regions of the present-day Indian States of Kerala and Karnataka.

De Rivier Palembangh

Stadt Palembangh

De Rivier Jambi

De Zee

there were any Dutch, they would immediately go there with a mighty fleet, and if one had no help or protection from land then, it would be dangerous to be there.

From this discourse it can be seen of what importance Melaka is; therefore we should well risk a black eye over it, for we have to have a permanent residence in the [East] Indies anyway,[323] and one may consider how much that would cost before it would be as suitable as Melaka.

---

323   A reference to the rendezvous.

Document 3

Excerpt of a letter by Matelieff to Admiral
Paul van Caerden
dated 4 January, 1608

[In late December 1607, the *Gelderland*[325] arrived at Banten with an urgent letter from the Gentlemen Directors, instructing VOC servants to set commercial interests aside and focus on the war effort against the Iberian powers. Around this time, Admiral Paul van Caerden arrived at Banten on his outbound journey from Europe, Mozambique and India. The two Dutch admirals exchanged views in person and in written form. In this letter to Van Caerden, Matelieff mentions the Directors' new instructions brought with the *Gelderland* and provides a sweeping overview of the security situation in different parts of East and Southeast Asia. A significant portion of the letter is dedicated specifically to discussing the situation in Johor as well as the potential for succeeding in a fresh military attack on Portuguese Melaka. The Malukus (especially Ternate), China and the Philippines take up the remaining sections of this epistolary brief.]

... First, the Directors say and expressly wish that if

---

325   The *Gelderland* had set sail with the fleet of Admiral Van
       Caerden. A Dutch-language transcript of these instructions
       have been published in De Booy, *De Derde Reis*, II,121.

Melaka has not been conquered by myself or Van Caerden, then Van Caerden should secure the settlement of Johor,[326] fortify it and station men there.

This pleases me very much, for as long as the Portuguese have the people of Johor as their enemies, in my opinion they will try no further. Had I not been obliged to go to the Malukus, and if the Directors had known and I had been allowed to break off my journey to China, I would have had a great appetite for this matter, of which I have often spoken. Now you have to make your reckoning whether it would be better in Johor[327] (the Johor River, that is) or on Bintan.[328] The Johor River is an excellent location, Bintan is unknown to me. If one could have a safe place for the ships on Bintan, it would not be bad there, but the Johor River is not to be despised either. Bintan lies in good sailing waters and from land one can see all the ships passing by in its vicinity. You should also take into account the means and power of the Portuguese, and the means and power of the Malays as well. I taught the Malays to fortify their city and they promised to do it. Then what? They do not want to work: as soon as I had gone, they left the work as it was. The great King [Ala'udin] drinks a lot, the *orang kaya* favor the Portuguese, Raja Seberang has no power, he dare not command the noblemen, the noblemen do not want him as their king, for then they would not have as much power as they have now; so

---

326 A reference to Batu Sawar, which was sometimes called Johor or New Johor in or on maps of this era. The term place or settlement employed here by Matelieff in the sense of the Malay term *negeri*.

327 The location of the proposed fort was in the lower reaches of the Johor River, around the former capital at Johor Lama. See also the list of place names *(Johor Lama)*.

328 One of the principal islands of the Riau Archipelago located south of the Singapore Strait. In the 16th and 17th centuries, Bintan served as a base of the *orang laut* as well as intermittently as the royal residence of the Johor rulers.

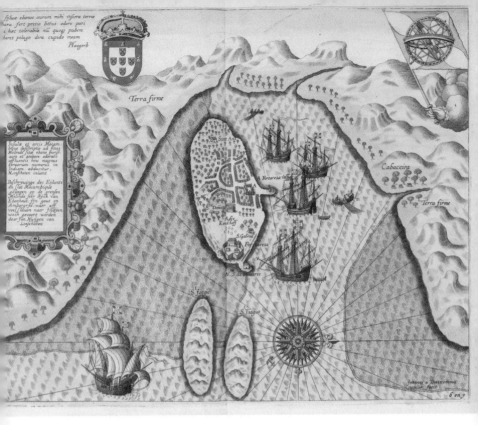

Hand-colored map of the Portuguese fort and settlement on Mozambique Island taken from the first edition of Jan Huyghen van Linschoten's Itinerario and Reysgeschrift, 1595-6. (The Hague: Royal Library, special collections, 1790 A 22, vol. I, after p. 6).

things stay in between. But I suspect that if you propose to them that you will leave men there, keep ships there and will live and die with them, that they will take courage then. All the more so because the Directors promise to send a strong armada this year,[329] which will also give them courage. Furthermore you may rest assured that neither the people of Johor nor any other blacks will resist the whites; if we sometimes see that they resisted the whites, like André Furtado

---

329   The armada of Admiral Pieter Willemsz. Verhoeff. These ships arrived in the Johor River estuary in January 1609.

[de Mendonça] at Johor and Viceroy Dom Martim Alfonso de Castro at Aceh, I think that was more because of disorder among the whites than because of the blacks' courage. For the Portuguese have a way of contempting the blacks, as we do the Portuguese at sea, which often turns out to be harmful; but if the people of Johor have a Dutch garrison, do not doubt that they will become a bit more courageous. Raja Seberang is wonderfully inclined towards us, in my opinion one can trust him. The bendahara and laksamana are pro-Portuguese and none of the great king's noblemen can be counted on. In my view, one ought to fortify Johor,[330] but in these months of January and February to pay attention in the first place to the ships that will come with cargo from China. For out of the six galleons that we encountered there, I guess that four will come back—for one will go to Japan in the coming year and the other was a merchant ship which had come from Siam. So if you can get behind them with your fleet, Melaka and Macao[331] would become greatly distressed. Having built yourself a fort on the Johor River or on Bintan, you should leave two of the fastest ships there, which could industriously patrol the Straits of Kundur[332] and Singapore together with the perahus from Johor, so that no victuals were to reach the city of Melaka. One should take care that the ships are cleaned every month to keep them in good sailing condition, to prevent any ships from escap-

---

330 Read: Batu Sawar.

331 Portuguese settlement and colony in China on the right bank of the Pearl River. Macao today is a Special Administrative Region of China.

332 An important maritime artery that connects the southern Melaka Strait with maritime routes to ports in eastern Sumatra, northern Java, and destinations in the eastern regions of the Indonesian Archipelago, including Makassar, the Banda Islands, the Malukus and Timor. It extends along the western coast of Karimun and Kundur Islands in present-day Kepulauan Province, Indonesia.

ing us. For if you could destroy the ships lying at anchor at Melaka presently, two ships will suffice to keep the Strait near Melaka under control. You are in friendly country everywhere there—Kedah, Perak, Aceh, and Aru—but trust the blacks [only for] as long as you are too strong for them. Otherwise, if they see an advantage in betraying you they will do so. As long as you remain the superior of the Portuguese at sea, all will worship you.

The contract I made with the king of Johor is with the merchants of the Johor factory.[333] I had given my secretary, Abraham van den Broeck, some conditions to negotiate with the king of Johor, and brought him to Pahang to travel to Johor. Laying siege to Melaka is no small matter, for the enemy will have fortified it greatly and one would first have to distress it gradually at sea, so that our fleet that will sail from our country in 1607 would find the city[334] in a state of distress; for attacking it by land from guard ships is not wise. In the meantime the kings of Pahang, Perak, Kedah, Indragiri, Jambi and Aceh will prepare to help on land; you have to address them all from now on. The king of Pahang promises help....

---

333   Read: the VOC factory at Batu Sawar.

334   Read: Batu Sawar

Document 4

Excerpts from a letter by Matelieff to the next Admiral arriving from Europe, dated 28 January, 1608

[Written just shortly before embarking on his return voyage to Europe, Admiral Matelieff left this epistolary brief to the next Dutch fleet commander to arrive at Banten. In this document, he urged his successor to pay special attention to the developments on Ternate (especially in relation to Fort Orange at Malayur which Matelieff had founded in the preceding year 1607), as well as in Johor, whose ruler had been placed under great pressure and duress by Portuguese Melaka.]

My lord Admiral,

I do not deem it necessary to narrate in detail the events of my entire journey—at Melaka and in the Malukus as well as in China—since there are people living here in Banten and in all the towns of the East-Indies who accompanied me and who can relate those events orally. This letter will only serve to [word missing] my opinion of their sequel. There are two things which one should attend to, as the state of Ternate, Johor and all requires. For Ternate must be relieved

Left: Printed etching of a Dutch attack on Palembang by D. de Jong, 1779-1805, partial view. Rijksmuseum Amsterdam, RP-B-OP-47.821.

before a fleet arrives from Manila,[335] and likewise Johor must be relieved before any force arrives from India, or the king will make an agreement with the enemy. For he is unable to carry on, since the noblemen do not pay any attention to the king, the Yang di Pertuan, and do not want to fortify the city at his bidding; and because he is a drunkard, he has no order among his people, for he pays no attention to anything but drinking and his women. If he wanted, within a month his city would be so strong that he could go to sleep without a worry, but there is no order or respect, and there will be none as long as no company of white men stays in the city of Batu Sawar. For the Malays have no faith in themselves and dare not let the enemy come up to their city. But I think Raja Seberang would have a bit more authority with 70 or 80 whites staying there, and the nobility (which favors the Portuguese) would not dare reveal itself and would be forced to fortify the city....

... After that, Admiral van Caerden arrived on the 5th of this month;[336] what I discussed with him you will find in the letters with this one, which I wrote to him at the roadstead here and halfway to Jeyakerta. He originally intended to go to Johor[337] to wait for the ships coming from China and to help Johor, but the wind was contrary to his plans and would have cost him much time. He would have been unable to make it in time, or the ships from China would have been at Melaka already; and then they would also have missed their [word missing] to sail to the Malukus, and would have been like an ass starving between two hay stacks. He therefore sailed to Ternate, may the Lord God grant him victory. He lost too much time to be able to stop here. In that time he

---

335   Here and subsequently, possibly also used in the sense of the Philippines in general.

336   5 January, 1608.

337   Read: Batu Sawar.

could have done great damage to the enemy, but the chance of that is gone. One should depart from our country earlier in spring....

... I think that with his arrival, Ternate will remain in good state. Therefore the first admiral coming here should make his way to Johor and Melaka to see if one could drive the enemy away from there. The surrounding kings will help as much as they can, but it should all be done gradually, so that their help is ready. Moreover, a large force is needed to bombard and storm Melaka, for it was a strong place already and has now been much fortified; nor will it ever be without ships now. The best attack will be by water, cutting off all their victuals that may come from outside. If there is no way to lay siege to Melaka on land, one should fortify Johor and leave men there to go privateering and distress Melaka while always having a safe place to retreat. As long as the enemy is kept busy there, he will not think of this route to Ternate, but anything he can do will have to be done via Manila, which is inconvenient for them.

But here, we now have this to worry about: that the ships coming from China, with their own men and those from Melaka, may well stop at Johor before a fleet comes from Holland. And the king, seeing that no ships have arrived for so long, might well listen to a peace proposal, like the old king has already started to do, and thus surrender our men at the request of the Portuguese. The queen of Patani would follow his example, for it is certain that if the people of Johor make peace, all the others such as Pahang, Patani, Jambi, Perak, Kedah and Aceh will make peace as well. But I definitely trust them to change their minds nonetheless as soon as new Dutch ships arrive. [Some words missing] we could bring our capital that is at hand there to safety. Therefore, as soon as the *Gouda*[338] arrives here—which should be any day

---

338   The *Gouda* had set sail with the fleet of Van Caerden in Decem-

now if the ship has not come to harm—I will send it to Johor and Patani, see how things stand there and have the money taken from the factories at Johor and Patani.

At Johor 10,000 reales[339] are at hand, 28,000 [pounds of] sandalwood[340] and then the outstanding debts, which are many at Patani: over 60,000 reales and about 50,000 [pounds of] sandalwood.[341] If I were not concerned for the capital, I would not worry about it much even if Johor made peace, for as soon as we returned with force that would change their minds again. We will not achieve anything profitable there unless we leave a hundred men there; then he will fortify his city.

I would advise against laying siege to Melaka, unless one could put ashore at least 1,200 men; but beginning again and then leaving the matter unfinished would be unwise. I think the people of Johor and the others will conduct more trade than they did in my time, but all these blacks are too slow in their business, which is strange. All the kings must be warned two months ahead, which can hardly be done without the Portuguese taking their measures as well. But in the meantime, one should [patrol] the sea near Melaka. This is the present state of the Indies, which may change yet before the first admiral arrives from our country....

... I would not worry about China unless Johor had been fortified first, for we will always manage to trade if only we have a place here[342] from which we can damage the

---

ber 1606 and had arrived in Aceh in January 1608.

339   Presumably reals-of-eight, equivalent to about 271 kilograms of coin-grade silver.

340   This corresponds to about 13.83 metric tons.

341   Presumably reals-of-eight, equivalent to about 1,620 kilograms of coin-grade silver. The weight of the sandalwood amounts to about 24.7 metric tons.

342   A reference by Matelieff on the urgency of establishing a ren-

Portuguese. So far we do not have a single place in the whole of the Indies where we can build our warehouse to protect the victuals and ships' maintenance, which we need badly. Here at Banten everything is cramped and difficult, we need a place where we are in control a bit more and where we can have people come and live from our country. When it comes to the Company's best interest, even if we had Johor, it is quite a bit out of the way; Banten or Jeyakerta would be the most useful to us. The king of Banten, I guess, does not want to have our presence so strong in his city. The king of Jeyakerta may speak beautifully now, but they are blacks and change every hour....

---

dezvous. See also the glossary *(rendezvous)*.

Document 5

Excerpts from Matelieff's Memorial of 12 November, 1608, entitled Discourse on the State of the East Indies

[This memorial provides a sweeping overview of the security and trading situation in Southeast Asia in general, as well as specifically in selected ports around the Malay Peninsula, China and the Indonesian Archipelago. Matelieff advanced several recommendations for the VOC that include the optimization of timing for fleet departures from Europe to Asia; the inadequacy of Banten as a principal base; the need to establish a rendezvous or permanent base in Asia; as well as the intricacies of forging diplomatic relations with Asian rulers. With specific reference to the Singapore-Johor nexus, Matelieff reported on several issues relating to Johor's military security, a recent Portuguese blockade and attack, as well as Batu Sawar's role as a marketplace for pepper.]

... Now let us go back to Johor and see that we keep the Portuguese busy there (so that they will lose their appetite for thinking about the Malukus and Banda), while we quarrel with them over the Chinese, Coromandel and Bengal trade, bringing Cambay into it as well. We should first of

Left: East Indiamen by H.C. Vroom, c.1600-1630. Rijksmuseum Amsterdam, SK-A-3108.

all seek to fortify the city of Johor;[343] I have attempted that earlier,[344] but after I had left for the Malukus everything has declined. Because [the king of Johor][345] had not strengthened his city, the Portuguese have come, and out of fear he has left his city and fled inland, setting fire to his city himself.[346] But the Portuguese never came upstream far enough to reach the city. Meanwhile, he has made a peace treaty with the Portuguese (I have seen the treaty)[347] which one should not take seriously, for as soon as I had sent the *Erasmus*[348] to Johor, he no longer cared for it.[349]

We therefore ought to try fortifying the city first; this would not work without using some harsh words, or else

343   Read: Batu Sawar

344   The date indicated is 18 September, 1606. The fortification of the royal residence Batu Sawar is mentioned as the first of four demands made by Matelieff. See similarly Jacques l'Hermite de Jonge's second letter to his father which is featured as an appendix to Matlieff, "Historische Verhael", BV, III, p. 173. The date provided in Commelin has been erroneously given as 18 September, 1607.

345   Read: King Ala'udin.

346   Earlier stories reported in Matelieff's *Journael* (entry of 30 December, 1607) claimed that the Portuguese had launched a naval campaign against Aceh with two galleys and 20 foists over a period of six weeks, and that Johor had been set ablaze.

347   This treaty, unfortunately, no longer survives.

348   See CMJ, 68.

349   Matelieff's *Journal* reported that Martin Aep (Apius) was dispatched on the *Erasmus* to Johor in November 1607. Apius expressed concern that the Johor monarch was about to make peace with the Portuguese and even managed to procure a copy of the draft clauses. One article reportedly held that the Johor monarch was to surrender any Dutchman to the Portuguese authorities. As Apius was not of the opinion that the peace was to take effect, Matelieff resolved that priority should be given to the fortification of the Malukus over Johor. See CMJ, 101, 271n90.

in such a way as would be best put into practice, not discussed in writing. The young king, Raja Seberang,[350] would be favorably inclined to this; the old one[351] is more capable of drinking than of ruling.[352] It would cost us 4,000 or 5,000 reals,[353] but if we made the investment we could collect it in due course; or if that went badly, we would still set the enemy back with it to such a degree that it would be of much greater importance to us. We should see if the situation is still as it was when I was there. Keeping a big garrison there would bring high costs with it; but after fortifying the city, the Malays would be somewhat reassured. Once the city has been reconstructed, we could reassure the Malays with 50 or 60 white soldiers, so that they would stay together and be alright; unless there came an army larger than I imagine can be called up from the Indies.

One ought to keep two or three ships or yachts around Melaka, which would harass navigation from Melaka with help from the Malays, who would well serve this purpose with their perahus and galleys. They would also encourage the king of Johor to keep ships in sight around his city at all times....

... But I would always buy pepper at Jeyakerta at a quarter of a real-of-eight coin[354] more than at Banten. This would have to be an arrangement for the time being and it would

---

350 The "young king" is a close translation from the Malay "Raja Bongsu".

351 Read: King Ala'udin.

352 Ala'udin Ri'ayat Shah of Johor, the elder (half-) brother of Raja Bongsu, and titular monarch of Johor, has been earlier described in Matelieff's *Journal* as an inept drunkard.

353 This is most likely a reference to reals-of-eight; the sums indicated would be equivalent to about 108 and 135 kilograms of coin-grade silver.

354 About 6.75 grams of coin-grade silver.

have to be done with finesse; or if one would not want to do that, one might (in the hope of a good outcome) do them a favor worth so much or more, so that one would drive all the trade there. This would have to be done skillfully at first; exactly how, would become clear in time. I think that over time the Indians could also bring as much pepper to our community there as the Company would need. But for now, one should still keep a clerk and two assistants at Johor, until one would see where the Johor cause was going. So I conclude that as far as pepper is concerned, Jeyakerta and Banten with the addition of Johor should bring us enough pepper for the time being, without our having to keep a factory at Aceh and Patani for that purpose; for it would certainly be brought to us at Jeyakerta and Johor, both by the Indians and by Dutch private merchants, as much as we would need....

The Johor factory:[355] as far as trade is concerned, I cannot think of a reason why it is profitable for us to keep an office for the Company there, for no goods whatsoever are produced there and all that was taken aboard there so far was a bit of pepper, which would get to Java in any case. But seeing how things stand in the war,[356] one might retain the factory there a bit longer. This is equally a location for trade by private merchants, but it does not cover the expenses....

---

355 The Dutch factory was located at Batu Sawar.

356 The war between the Dutch Republic and the Iberian powers Spain and Portugal.

Document 6

Excerpt from Matelieff's memorial written after 12 November, 1608, entitled Discourse on Trade Possibilities for the VOC in the East Indies

[This memorial was written by Matelieff after his return to the Dutch Republic in September 1608. It was also written after the "Discourse on the State of the East Indies" which is dated 12 November, 1608. In this document, Matelieff provided a sweeping overview of trading opportunities in Southeast Asia and the Indian Subcontinent. With specific reference to the Singapore-Johor nexus, this memorial is an important source for understanding the dynamics of Johor's trade of raw diamonds from Sambas on Borneo.]

... If the king of Johor stayed—he has a place there, I believe at the river called Sambas,[357] which belongs to Raja

---

357   A river and polity in southwestern Borneo in present-day Indonesia. The king of Sambas, who controlled the river, its tributary and upstream towns was a vassal (or client; he actually signed himself with the title *adipati* or governor) of Johor, specifically however of Raja Bongsu. The VOC concluded a treaty with Sambas in October 1610. For an English translation of this treaty, see CMJ, 446-8. Additional information about Sambas contained in a report by Samuel Bloemaert, touching

Seberang—we would be safe there, and let the [diamonds] be brought there from upriver. An argument against this, however, would be that the king of Johor, who is very greedy, would want to shear the sheep and let us shear the pigs.[358] One ought to make a deal with him; if, alternatively, it could be done without involving him, that would be more profitable but less safe. One should find an occasion to discuss it with the king of Johor and see what his inclinations are in this matter. Without that, I cannot make a definite assessment, for it is a merchandise of which one carries 100,000 guilders'[359] worth in one hand without the other hand knowing about it. This is an occasion for sin, and the gentlemen know well that if death had not been a good controller, many or indeed most of the stones which are brought to them now would not have given them much trouble to sort, for they would have been sorted, sold and delivered without them....

---

on its trade in diamonds, bezoar stones and gold, the role of Chinese trade, as well as its poor political relations with up-stream tributary regions in Landak, is found within the main of Admiral Verhoeff's voyage to Asia. See BV, III, "Journael ende Historische Verhael... van de Reys.... gedaen door Pieter Willemsz. Verhoeff...", 98-102, esp. 100-1.

358 This is as much as to say as the king of Johor takes the lion's share of the profits and leaves slim pickings to the Dutch.

359 About 1,070 kilograms of coin-grade silver.

Document 7

Excerpt of Matelieff's Memorial to Hugo Grotius and Johan van Oldenbarnevelt, dated 31 August, 1610

[In this memorial, the admiral commented on the instructions of the VOC directors to look into the establishment of a rendezvous in the region of the Johor River estuary. The location the directors had in mind was around present-day Tanjung Pengerang located on the Johor mainland across from Singapore's Changi Point. Matelieff explained that this location was not suitable because, unlike locations along the northwest coast of Java close to the Sunda Strait, the Johor River estuary could not be reached at all times of the year. Moreover, the kings of Johor—and that meant King Ala'udin Ri'ayat Shah III as well as Raja Bongsu—were clearly not disposed to grant the Dutch permission to construct a fortress at a location around the river estuary. The admiral also touched on a range of other issues, including the prospects of conquering Banda and acquiring Muslim subjects, political problems at Banten, Jeyakerta and Ternate, as well as Johor, Patani, Kedah, China and Japan. He explained the drawbacks of the fleet commander system (citing specifically the example of Verhoeff's problematic negotiations in Johor) and cautioned that the stationing of soldiers and garrisons across the Indies would prove too costly for the VOC.] [360]

Dear Sir,

I have informed you several times earlier, both in writing and in person, as well as my poor abilities allowed, of the situation in the East Indies; in which I think I have fulfilled my duty and merely done as I am obliged to, and I intended to bother you no more about it. It has come to my attention, however, that the Gentlemen Directors in their latest instruction to Governor-[General] Pieter Both have indicated the Hook of Johor to him as the place to keep his residence (as a consequence, that would become our rendezvous). I then did not think it necessary to write to you against it, since it was sufficiently rebutted in my previous writings, before that instruction had been written. Moreover, the Gentlemen Directors have been informed with the latest arriving ships that the king of Johor is completely opposed to creating a fortress in his country, so that need will make us understand what we cannot understand by reason. Because the Seventeen[361] are meeting again now, and I shall be in attendance on some matters which concern me in particular, I suppose that they will speak of the government of the state of the Indies again there, and that by experience one will understand some things better than before. Fearing none-

---

360   The Hague, National Archives of the Netherlands, *Collectie Hugo de Groot Supplement* (1.10.35.02, no. 40), fols. 524-31. Full transcripts of this document are also found in Frederiks, "Cornelis Cornelisz Matelieff de Jonge en zijn geslagt," *Rotterdamsche Historiebladen,* 3 afd., 1.1 (1871): 328-36 as well as in Henk J.M. Nellen, ed., *Briefwisseling van Hugo Grotius,* zeventiende deel, Supplement 1583-1645, with the addenda compiled by C.M. Ridderikhoff (The Hague: Instituut voor Nederlandse Geschiedenis, 2001), no. 198A, 71-5; see also CMJ, 344-52.

361   That is the central board of directors of the VOC. See also CMJ, 481.

DOCUMENT 7

theless that they might stay with their old opinion, I could not stop myself from putting in writing for you some considerations on the government of the Indies, so that if necessary, you can hold up to them what you shall find pertinent to its prosperity.

First, the rendezvous at Johor is unsuitable, because one cannot reach it every time of the year. It is also unsuitable to navigate and sail to all locations, and then there is the jealousy of the aforementioned king who does not want to concede us a fortress there, as I and Pieter Willemsz. [Verhoeff] after me have found out by experience.[362] Taking Banda is not very profitable to us without further arrangements, for we do not possess it very completely and still we keep the reputation that we have subdued the people. This has earned us the disapproval of the neighboring kings, who no longer believe our old phrase that we are only after business and not after conquering land. Our first arrival made us welcome, when we said that we wanted to destroy the dominion of the Portuguese, but now we invade the lands ourselves and treat the people worse than the Portuguese do, in Ambon for instance, where we have supremacy. Then there are the great costs which Banda will involve for us, and our nation's inexperience in governing the Muhammadans;[363] so that we shall not manage Banda well and make great expenses there, just as in Ambon, which can be managed better at a third of the expenses than is done presently.

In Ternate, there should be many more people than there are now, and trade in everything should be made more copious than is happening now. The most important thing of all: the rendezvous should be established at a location which is not subject to monsoon or adverse winds when coming from these lands. I cannot think of a better place than in the Strait of Sunda or Banten, some 20 miles further or closer

362   See Document 8.
363   Read: Muslims.

155

Printed etching of the Dutch statesman Johan van Olden-barnevelt, one of the intended recipients of Matelieff's memorials. Peter Borschberg, private collection.

than Banten. We can always get there well enough, once we have rounded the Cape of Good Hope.

But the difficulties to achieve that are growing by the day and one will have much more difficulty now than before to establish it, for I had an eye on the islands of Jeyakerta, which are very well situated for fortification as well as good locations from which to manage everything. We should do that with the consent of Banten and Jeyakerta, as I have explained in my previous writings. But now the king of

Jeyakerta[364] has been strengthened by the temenggong of Banten and the shahbandar, who have brought no less than 2,000 men with them from Banten to Jeyakerta. This has made him a bit stronger and not as easy to deal with as before, as the signs are already revealing. But we should make such a deal with the two aforementioned kings that we are allowed to have our rendezvous there and make them understand that it is profitable—there certainly are ways to do this without damage to us, too long to narrate in writing....

The king of Johor, who is our friend, is being reduced to misery because of our friendship. Moreover, the pepper his land produces is transported to Patani and bought at a higher price by us there than in Johor. Thus we deprive him of trade while we ought to do the opposite, and we drive the trade toward the people of Patani, who have none themselves and who make us pay as much toll as they want....

It is also a big mistake of the Gentlemen Directors that they have sent new commanders to the Indies every year, for the new one always wants to denounce or correct the work that had been done. But because of his inexperience, he often understands little of what his predecessor has done, who has been in the Indies longer than he and knows the Indians' inclinations best; like it has happened with the king of Johor, with whom Admiral Pieter Willemsz. [Verhoeff] wanted to make a different agreement than I had made with him.[365] The king was dissatisfied with this and said that he had no wish to make a new agreement every day, and that whoever came after him, Pieter Willemsz. [Verhoeff], would want to make yet another agreement. Therefore, one must make a good arrangement and then continue on that basis, instead of something new every day.[366] I see no way to keep

---

364 That is Pangerang Wijayakrama, alias Prince Jeyawikarta.

365 See document 8.

366 This loosely quotes a sentence from the letter of Ala'udin Ri'ayat Shah and Raja Bongsu of Johor addressed to the King

many people in the Indies unless one realizes the things I have explained to the directors: allowing people from these lands who would come and live at our rendezvous to conduct inland trade freely there, like the Portuguese do with their people. As a consequence, we would draw all the trade away from the Portuguese and into our hands, and many Indians would come and live with us who now live under the neighboring kings but do the same trade nonetheless. I dare be so bold as to say that we would supply the nutmeg, mace and cloves at such a low price in our rendezvous as they now cost the directors. Then our ships sailing from the fatherland would only stay away for 18 months, and consequently [the men] would not die as they do every day now—something which a good patriot with good eyes cannot watch, but is obliged to remedy as much as he can, which also lends me the audacity to write this to you.

---

of Holland (i.e. the Stadholder and Gentlemen States General) dated 8 December, 1609. See document 11.

Document 8

Excerpt from the Log and Report

of all that was seen and all that happened on the voyage made by the honorable and righteous Pieter Willemsz. Verhoeff, admiral-general over 13 ships, to the East Indies, China, the Philippines and surrounding countries, in the year 1607 and the following years. All taken from the journals kept by Johan de Moelre, senior merchant on the lord admiral's ship, and Jacques le Febvere, fiscaal of the same fleet

[As Admiral Paul van Caerden had been unable to reach the Singapore Straits in January 1608 due to strong contrary winds, the next Dutch fleet to visit the Johor River towns was only a year later, namely during in the opening weeks of 1609. The ships placed under the supreme command of Pieter Willemsz. Verhoeff had set sail from the Dutch Republic on 21 December, 1607, and after rounding the Cape of Good Hope, attacked the Portuguese fort on Mozambique Island. Later, Verhoeff menaced Goa, sailed down the Malabar Coast toward Calicut, and headed from there toward the Malay Peninsula. After ascertaining that a fresh attack on Portuguese Melaka was not feasible, he proceeded to the Singapore Straits and the Johor River

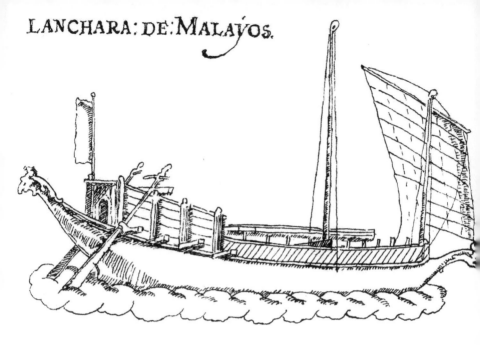

LANCHARA: DE MALAYOS.

Hand drawn illustration of a Malay lanchara or lancha. Taken from Manuel Godinho de Erédia's Declaraçam de Malaca *(Description of Melaka), c. 1613.*

estuary. The Dutch fleet dropped anchor off Johor Lama during the final days of the Muslim month of Ramadan in January 1609. From here, the admiral and several of his leading officers transferred to smaller vessels to sail upstream to Batu Sawar. The excerpt from the log of Verhoeff's voyage picks up in late November, 1608, as the ships were approaching Melaka. With reference to the Singapore-Johor nexus, this translated excerpt is especially important as it provides a record of the negotiations that took place at the court of Batu Sawar, including Verhoeff's failed attempt to persuade King Ala'udin and Raja Bongsu to permit the construction of a Dutch fort in the region of the Johor River estuary.][367]

367   The full text has been published as "Journael ende Verhael Van alle het gene dat ghesien ende voor-ghevallen is op de Reyse, Gedaen door den E. ende Gestrengen Pieter Willemsz Verhoeven, Admirael Generael over 13. Schepen, gaende near de Oost-Indien, China, Philipines ende byleggende Rijcken, In den Iare 1607. Ende volgende...." in BV,

On the 24th [of November, 1608] … Pieter Gerritsz., skipper of the Amsterdam,[368] was sent with letters to the merchant of Johor or Batu Sawar[369] with two well-manned yachts (as decided) to inform the king of their arrival and to offer fulfilment of the agreement made with Admiral Cornelis Matelieff to lay siege to the city of Melaka by sea, if it pleased His Majesty[370] to carry this out by land.[371] The merchant was ordered to motivate His Majesty for this and encourage him to obtain this assistance, doing everything to persuade His Majesty. He was also ordered to provision the fleet with rice and arak.[372]

On the 25th of that month, the admiral and the broad council sailed to the island where the sloops were being constructed, as a frigate from the mainland had moored there with about 40 people on board: men, women and children, natives of Pegu,[373] who requested protection from the

---

III, 1-214 (separate foliation). The section translated here corresponds to p. 38-45 of this early modern printed text. A transcript of this section is also found in Opstall, *De reis*, I, 242–56.

368 This ship, and other vessels mentioned in this document, belonged to the fleet of Admiral Pieter Willemsz. Verhoeff.

369 Read: Abraham van den Broeck.

370 Read: Ri'ayat Shah III.

371 Reference is here to the Johor-Dutch Treaty of 17 May 1606. See p. 98-102 in this book.

372 An alcoholic beverage, usually the fermented (or distilled) juice of the wild nipa palm. According to Erédia, the "wild palm called 'Nypeiras' resemble the palms of India in shape and leaf" highlighting that they are "somewhat bigger" than date palm. "They have a big, stump base and grow in the swampy land." Nipa palm wine, he further observed was "most esteemed" among the Malays. See JDC, p. 301-2; MGED, 20, 27, 29.

373 From present-day Myanmar.

tyranny of the Portuguese. They were thus allowed access to the island. They furthermore stated that the Portuguese were very busy strengthening their position at Melaka, that most of the noblemen had begun to flee with their women and children, and that there were no more than 400 soldiers inside, apart from the casados.[374] About two hours after sunset, those in the fort fired three cannon shots, charged with muskets[375] and beat the drums.

On the 26th, skipper Willem Jacobsz. was ordered to take the western route with his ship *Zeelandia* and occupy the narrow of the Strait [of Melaka], in order to look out for a ship with pieces of cloth which was expected from São Tomé any time.

In the morning of the 27th, with the dawn there arrived from Melaka four frigates,[376] two lancharas[377] and other ships, up to 36 in number, and by surprise attacked the island where the Dutch were constructing their yachts. The *Roode Leeuw*,[378] keeping watch and sighting them, fired a shot, but those on the island did not pay attention because of bad supervision, so that they could land easily. Finding the guard posts badly kept, they attacked them, killed several and drove the rest to the seaside. Then they started pillaging, which made the Dutch take heart and confront the Portuguese with few men, but full of courage, driving them back. The Portuguese left behind 23 dead and many

---

374 Married Portuguese settlers.

375 An armament fired from the shoulder; a precursor of the modern rifle. See JDC, 330.

376 The term originally refers to an open Portuguese naval craft that was often rowed and in the 16th and 17th century, was deployed in the East Indies. See JDC, 322.

377 These terms refer to small Asian vessels that were propelled by breast oars and could also be sailed. See the illustration on 160, and JDC, 305, 327; SMS, 333.

378 Lit. "Red Lion".

wounded, and had to drag three of their captains with them. The Dutch casualties were Captain Huybert Scheurmans, his sergeant and three common soldiers; three were wounded and three taken prisoner. When the men in the fleet heard of this, they came to their people's help, convened the broad council and decided to quarter all the soldiers on the island to prevent incidents of this kind in the future.

In the afternoon of the 28th [of November], 13 orang laut[379] (who are freebooters[380] and subjects of the king of Johor), staying on the Melakan shores to harm the Portuguese, came aboard the admiral's ship.[381] The captains and officers came to Admiral [Verhoeff] and told him that they had left Johor two weeks earlier: there had been no Dutch ships there at the time, nor any news of their coming, but they had encountered the yachts on the way by chance. Furthermore, a letter to the merchant of Johor[382] was drawn up and dispatched there with one of the said orang laut.

On December 1, a Frenchman originating from La Rochelle defected from Melaka and informed the admiral of the whole situation, saying that the city was well provided, with 35 large cannons, gunpowder, lead and provisions.

On the 2nd of the same month, a soldier was keel-hauled on the admiral's ship because he intended to defect at Mozambique and had persuaded others to do the same.

In the morning of the 3rd, some sails were sighted at sea. The admiral therefore dispatched Jan Walichsz. with the

---

379 Orig. *saletten,* i.e. saletes or selates; lit. "people of the straits".

380 Orig. *vrijbuyters.* It is noted that the orang laut are not labelled as pirates, but as freebooters, which offers an important legal distinction. Piracy is an illegal activity, freebooting is conducted under the laws of war and skirts the border between acceptable and non-acceptable.

381 Admiral Verhoeff's flagship.

382 Van den Broeck.

Roode Leeuw[383] and two armed boats to survey the said sails. In the evening they returned to the fleet, bringing one of the said sails with them: a Javanese junk with 40 men and a cargo of rice, poultry, pepper, arak and dried fish, which was taken over by the fleet. The men thanked them, since they claimed that they were our friends and on their way to Johor.

On the 5th, another Javanese junk was taken with a cargo that was unloaded and paid for as before.

On the 7th, the junior merchant of the ship *Zeelandia* (which was keeping watch at Cape Rachado) arrived at the fleet and reported that on the morning of the 6th, they had chased a ship of about 40 lasts[384] with their ship and boat; when they approached it, the enemy hit them hard, firing mightily with large cannons and muskets. A man's leg was shot to pieces and he died shortly afterwards. Thus they were forced to leave, repair the boat and man it afresh. After that, they sailed back to the prize but staying under their ship's cover all the time. When the enemy noticed this and saw no way out, they set fire to the ship at about 1 ½ miles[385] north of Cape Rachado in the evening and rowed away from it with their canoe, so that it was completely burnt.[386]

In the afternoon, the men of the fleet sighted two sails, the *Geunieerde Provincien*[387] and two manned boats were thus sent there. In the evening, they brought back the news that both were sloops[388] that had been at Johor or Batu Sawar with Pieter Gerritsz. [The men of the fleet also said that they] had chased two ships with a cargo of cloves and

---

383   Lit. "Red Lion".
384   About 80 tons.
385   The distance here is presumably given in Dutch sea-miles— around 10 kilometers.
386   The orig. reads lit. "burnt to the ground".
387   Lit. "United Provinces".
388   A single-masted sailing boat featuring a lateen mainsail and a headsail.

Contemporary picture of Radix China or China Root. Peter Borschberg, private collection. Scale in centimetres.

rice. From the ships, a bale of rice and a bale of cloves had been thrown overboard. The yachts had picked them up and brought them aboard the admiral's ship. The yachts *Pauw*[389] and *Grijphioen*[390] were then ordered to the aforementioned prizes, and after them the ships *Hoorn*[391] and *Geunieerde Provincien* as well, following a resolution of the broad council. One of these was to sail south-south-west, the other west-south-west, in order to sight the said prizes in case they escaped the yachts under cover of the night. In the morning, they saw the yachts and sloops chasing the one prize. The other was discovered by the big ships, which followed it northwest and took it. On the 11th, they returned to the fleet with both prizes, which had a very rich cargo of raw silk, velvets, damasks,[392] preserves, porcelain, China root,[393] pepper

---

389 Lit. "Peacock".

390 Lit. "Griffin".

391 A town in northern Holland.

392 A reversible fabric of cotton, silk or both. See JDC, 318.

393 A knotty rhizome of the Sarsaparilla family that found widespread application in the treatment of gout, skin disorders and to treat some symptoms of syphilis. See JDC, 336; SMS, 338; Borschberg, "The Euro-Asian Trade and Medicinal Usage of

and other goods. They measured about 60 lasts[394] each and had 110 persons on board, among them 40 Portuguese, the rest Chinese and Gujaratis, and three monks as well (they were all imprisoned on the ships). They were equipped with six light cannons, both brass and iron. The lord admiral and vice-admiral sailed over to them and had everything unloaded in an orderly fashion.

On the same date, they saw a canoe coming toward the fleet. The admiral then sent his little ship to it and a man was found in it with both legs chained. When he was interrogated, he had nothing to say but that a few days earlier the frigates from Melaka had chased some lancharas which had the merchant of Johor[395] on board, so that they were forced to fly to the shore and go into the woods, although some Johorese were killed and wounded. A little later, four bantins came alongside the admiral's ship with a letter from the aforementioned merchant of Johor, who was staying at about 4 miles from Melaka and asked the admiral for a yacht or two to come and fetch him, because the frigates were lying in wait for him. They also said that the king [of Johor] was to arrive in two or three days to discuss the Melaka matters with the admiral.

On the 12th, the yacht *Pauw* was dispatched to pick up the said merchant. On the same date the news arrived that at Macao in China, a large junk was being loaded in order to sail here with the monsoon. It was therefore decided that the ship *Roode Leeuw*, the yacht *Grijphioen* and the sloop of the ship *Amsterdam* would sail to Singapore Strait to wait for and seize the junk. On the same date, everyone was ordered to hand the loot from the last two prizes to the admiral. In the afternoon the yacht *Pauw* returned to the fleet, bringing

---

Radix Chinae," *Revista de Cultura*, International Edition, 20 (2006): 102-115. See also the illustration on 183.

394 About 120 tons.

395 Van den Broeck.

with it the aforementioned merchant of Johor, by the name of Abraham van den Broeck, former secretary to the Lord Admiral Cornelis Matelieff, who made him senior merchant and left him there.

On the 18th, the broad council resolved that since three monks had been taken on the last two prizes, they were to write to Melaka for their liberation on the condition that they would send three of their men and one of Matelieff's men whom they had taken prisoner. The letter was sent to the city with a Chinese, who returned by evening with a written reply which was communicated in the broad council on the 19th. It said that the [Portuguese] were willing to exchange our three prisoners for the said monks, but concerning the fourth man that they were negotiating with Sunda to exchange him for a great fidalgo[396] who was in prison there. On this count, it was decided that another important Portuguese would be offered for him, since it was assumed that they had taken him to Spain. But after long debates, the decision was taken to free all the Portuguese prisoners. One could not approve of killing them in cold blood because they had been taken prisoner in a just war. In this matter, Jan de Molre, Simon Jansz. Hoen and Pieter Hertsingh from Ilha Grande[397] were tasked with these prisoners. They put them ashore on the west side of Melaka and waited for our men from the city—all of which was duly accomplished.

The fleet took in fresh water at Ilha Grande, intending to continue its journey because they had information, from the royal envoy from Johor and the merchant Abraham van den Broeck as well as from the Malays, Klings[398] and other people who came from Melaka, that with 500 soldiers—the

---

396   A nobleman, a hidalgo.

397   Lit. "Big Island"; present-day Pulau Besar.

398   Persons from the south of India. The term is seen to represent a corruption of Kalinga, a Hindu kingdom.

casados, servants and slaves apart, a larger number than the aforementioned soldiers—not taking into account the Malays, Klings and other nations, the city was well provided with ammunition and provisions for a very long time. Its walls and bulwarks [were] of such disposition that they needed not fear their enemies, while they could do great damage themselves, having many large cannons, two of them of an extraordinary size and a very wide reach. Nor was the king of Johor able to give them much assistance by land, as had become apparent in Admiral Matelieff's time: they would be unable to muster more than 900 men on land, not enough to close in the city. They found it inadvisable, therefore, to attempt it.

They decided thus to leave from there and on the 29th, with a northeast wind, set a course for Johor. On January 5, 1609, they arrived at the entrance to the Singapore Strait,[399] a narrow strait to pass through (only one ship at a time can sail through). On the same date, the admiral, vice-admiral and some of his councilors left for Batu Sawar with four yachts to pay their respects to the king of Johor and give him a few presents. Two miles[400] after passing the aforementioned strait,[401] the Johor River begins. At the entrance there are hillocks or small islands resembling sugar cones,[402] one of them four times bigger than the other. The one is to north-north-east as one enters the [Johor] River,[403] the other north-

---

399   Judging by the description, this would have been at the western entrance to the Old Strait of Singapore, between present-day Labrador Park and Fort Siloso on Sentosa.

400   This is assumed to be expressed in Dutch sea miles; about 15 kilometers.

401   That is, the Old Strait of Singapore.

402   Refined sugar was sold in large cones (usually about 40-50 centimeters high) with rounded tops.

403   This is probably a reference to Bukit Belungkor.

east,[404] while on the other side of the river lies a hill [with a] mountain,[405] but on the southwestern side it is not so high.

In the early morning of the 8th, the lord admiral with his company and baggage transferred from his yachts to some perahus at Johor Lama in order to continue his journey to Batu Sawar. His Majesty, hearing of their arrival, sent some frigates with his highest nobility to meet them and greet them on His Majesty's behalf. In the afternoon, they arrived well and found a big elephant ready for them, on which the admiral and the vice-admiral sat to ride to His Majesty's court with all the merchants following on foot. Upon arriving there, they were solemnly welcomed by His Majesty and given their leave after little talk, since they were tired from the journey, and so they were brought to their lodgings.

On the 8th, the fleet arrived at the river of Old Johor[406] and dropped anchor at a depth of 9 fathoms.[407] In the morning, there was a big festival at Johor, which they celebrate only once a year.[408] Thus the lord admiral with his company went to see king Yang di Pertuan (the highest king) ride to church,[409] the three of them sitting on an elephant: in the middle, the king himself, Raja Seberang in front and another important gentleman behind, all in great state with a large retinue of noblemen. At the church, a highly ornate platform had been made, onto which His Majesty stepped off the elephant and went to church to attend his superstitious service there. Having done that, he climbed back onto the said elephant and rode to his court, having the lord admiral precede

---

404   Probably Bukit Pengerang (formerly known as Johor Hill).

405   The mountain is probably Bukit Pulai on the Johor mainland.

406   The Johor River. The name "Old Johor" refers to Johor Lama, the former capital and royal residence of Johor.

407   A little over 15 meters.

408   Eid al-Fitr, the end of the fasting month of Ramadan.

409   Read: mosque.

him with his men, who often blew the trumpets. Arriving there, he made his people sit in a circle in which the lord admiral and vice-admiral were also placed. After some talk with His Majesty, they were allowed to leave and go to their lodgings. In the afternoon, the presents to Yang di Pertuan were made as well as to Raja Seberang, who took the lord admiral and his company by the hand and went to seat them at a table set the Dutch manner. Here he entertained all of them in a very friendly way and (after some talk) they were served food in the way mentioned and made merry with the others. Halfway through the meal, two girls appeared and then danced very merrily to the sound of little drums and women's singing, which was strange and amusing to watch.

After that, because it was getting late, they took their leave from His Majesty, who showed them great friendship and had them accompanied to their lodgings by some noblemen.

On the 11th, both kings, Yang di Pertuan and Raja Seberang, seated in a beautifully decorated frigate, came before the Dutch lodgings and asked the lord admiral to join them, which he did (while the vice-admiral and other merchants boarded another frigate), sailing up the river together to view a certain city[410] which His Majesty was having newly built. Having returned to Batu Sawar, they stayed with King Yang di Pertuan for dinner that evening and were given their meal the Dutch way, but served exclusively by women.

In the evening of the 12th the lord admiral with his councilors was summoned to the king, whom they found in a meeting with his council. They therefore sat down there as well and explained the reason for their visit in the name of His Princely Excellency [Stadholder Maurice of Nassau], the Most Mighty Gentlemen States General as well as the Gentlemen Directors: to build a fort there [in Johor] for the defense of them all and the detriment of the Portuguese,

---

410   This was presumably Pasar (or Pasir) Raja.

their common enemy. To which His Majesty replied that he was not able to consent to that thus far; but should they be willing to help him with money and ammunition to keep up the war against the Portuguese, they would oblige him very much and give cause for a more enduring friendship.

On the same date, a certain seaman from the ship *Delft*, keeping watch in a yacht on the [Johor] River, went for a swim and was devoured by a caiman[411] so that nothing but a little of his bowels was found, which was a warning to all sailing persons not to go into the water for a swim lightly in an unknown place.

On the 13th, both kings, Yang di Pertuan and Raja Seberang, came to the fleet with their highest noblemen or orang kaya in two galleys and some frigates and waited for the lord admiral halfway. The next day, January 14, he went to meet them with his broad council and they went aboard together (while many cannons and muskets were fired). There they found everything much to their liking, and the Yang di Pertuan asked to be given a set of clothes made the Dutch way, and so he was. They were well received and treated, drinking to the health of Their Majesties and His Princely Excellency.

On the 15th, all the soldiers and some sailors were ordered to go ashore in armor with their officers and show a mock battle with each other, so that Their Majesties might see the manner of fighting which the Dutch employ in the open field. This amused them greatly.

On the 17th, the broad council was summoned aboard the admiral's ship and His Majesty's reply was communicated: thus far he had no intention to allow any fort to be built. Admiral Cornelis Matelieff had never requested anything of the sort, but had asked for help in conquering Melaka. The broad council then decided to deductively show His Majesty the great benefit that His Majesty would have

---

411   A type of crocodile.

from the building of the aforementioned fort, both in commerce and in defense against his enemies, the more so since His Majesty had no places which were able to withstand the Portuguese, his enemies, so that His Majesty's entire salvation or destruction was in the said fortress. To which His Majesty replied that they did not fear the Portuguese as much as they were believed to (although he knew that they had a big fleet at hand) because he and his people could always flee upriver. This they would not be able to do if the Dutch were there, because then they would be forced to help protect them, and thus his utter ruin could be near. [He said] that the Dutch were like the Portuguese, so that he feared that, if they came to live there in large numbers, they would have dealings with his subjects' women, as the Portuguese had done before. Then he would be forced to start a war against his friends, for neither he nor his men would ever tolerate any harm to be done to their women. Therefore, he could not grant their request as yet, but for now asked to be helped in his need with money and ammunition, and that it please the admiral and his councilors to come to Johor in person, since there were some secret issues to be discussed with them. It was thus decided that the lord admiral, vice-admiral, Johan de Molre and Groenewegen were to go there, which they did on the next day, the 18th, and arrived at night.

On the 19th, Raja Seberang and his most important councilors came to the lord admiral's house and stated, among other secret matters: "since the admiral did not have it in his power to reinstate him in his reign of Melaka and since his youngest brother, the king of Patani, had been robbed both of his kingdom and his life by the reigning queen (because of adultery with his concubine), so that he, the king of Johor, had a legal claim to the said kingdom—he wished to join forces with the admiral to expel the queen and divide her kingdom among themselves."[412]

---

412   Compare this story with the one told in document 10.

On the 21st of that month, the lord admiral and the councilors who accompanied him went to a banquet at His Majesty's and were each given a gold kris by Raja Seberang after the feast. The admiral, in return, presented His Majesty with his side gun (which he wanted badly), they swore oaths of loyalty to each other and after friendly goodbyes, they went to their lodgings and returned to the fleet on the 22nd.

On the 23th, the admiral summoned the broad council and noted that the king of Johor had become an enemy of the Portuguese because of his alliance with the Dutch and was in great need because of it. It was to be feared that after their departure [the king] would try to make peace with the Portuguese—much to the detriment of the Gentlemen Directors, their masters. [The admiral enquired] whether it would not be advisable to grant [the king] the assistance he requested so that this would not happen.

It was therefore decided unanimously that they would come to the aid of the aforementioned king, first with a sum of 3,000 reals-of-eight[413] deriving from the goods off the ships from Macao that had been captured near Cape Rachado; [414] then [they would also assist] with 20 barrels of gunpowder and some spelter or tintinago[415] to cast bullets. Finally [they would] leave two ships at the entrance of their rivers,[416] namely the ship *Roode Leeuw* and the yacht *Grijphioen*, to protect His Majesty's subjects, on the condition that they

---

413   About 87.2 kilograms of coin-grade silver.

414   Present-day Tanjung Tuan.

415   An alloy of copper and zinc and sometimes also lead. See JDC, 346–7; SMS, 338.

416   Other than the Johor River, it is not certain which other waterway might come in question here. As the Tebrau Strait was sometimes regarded as another arm of the Johor River in the late 16th and early 17th centuries, it may very well be a reference to this waterway. This means the two Dutch vessels would cruise the waters just off of present-day Changi Point, Pulau Ubin and Pulau Tekong Besar.

had free access to all his ports and were governed by the lord admiral's instructions.

On the 24th, Raja Seberang and some of his noblemen came to visit the admiral on his ship, where he spent the night and sailed back to land on the 25th.

On the 26th, the broad council decided that since there was a long journey ahead, every man would henceforth be given a wine ration of a *mutsken*[417] a day and on the ships where no butter was available, every man a mutsken of oil a week.

In the afternoon the yacht *Pauw* was ordered to weigh anchor and sail for Singapore Strait, where the ship *Roode Leeuw* and the yacht *Grijphioen* were keeping watch, to relieve the said yacht (since it had many sick on board). In the night, the admiral with some of his councilors sailed to Johor, taking with him the intended 3,000 reals-of-eight[418] to assist the king (in building his new city).

On the 27th, the yacht *Grijphioen* returned to the fleet on the river from its watch.

On the 29th, one of the sailors had a large piece of flesh bitten out of his side by a shark while he was swimming. Because of his loud screams he was still brought to safety, but died shortly afterwards. The said shark hung around the ships and did not swim away, so that it was caught in the end. It was as big as had not been seen on the entire voyage. After its belly had been cut open, the piece of flesh from the sailor was found inside and therefore buried with the sailor.

After the sick men from the yacht *Grijphioen* had been brought ashore to let them recuperate, a soldier from the ship *Zeelandia* joined them who behaved like a beast, turning against anyone. Finally he was met by one of the sick men (who was returning from a walk) and without saying a word treacherously stabbed him to death with a kris (which

---

417   About 0.15 liters.

418   About 87.2 kilograms of coin-grade silver.

he had stolen from a Malay), after which he fled to the forest without being caught. The admiral therefore placed a tael of gold[419] on his head and asked the king of Johor to punish him for his deed if [the culprit] fell into his hands, which the king promised to do.

On February 3, the lord admiral and his accompanying councilors returned to the fleet from Johor or Batu Sawar, having conducted his business there and taken his leave from both kings.[420] He left Jacques Obelaer there as senior merchant, Abraham Willemsz de Rijck as junior merchant and Hector Roos as diamond expert, with three assistants and a few other persons. He appointed the former merchant Abraham van den Broeck senior merchant on the ship *Roode Leeuw*. He further ordered the ship *Roode Leeuw* and the yacht *Grijphioen* to remain there in the [Johor] River estuary[421] until July 1 of that year to protect the aforementioned kings and their subjects, and then head for Patani, Borneo and finally [join with] the fleet in the Malukus. He likewise ordered them to transfer 20,000 reals-of-eight[422] to the ship *Hollandia*, and the yacht *Grijphioen* 10,000 reals to the ship Rotterdam.

On the 6th, they floated down the [Johor] River and once outside, dropped anchor at 10 fathoms' depth,[423] from where they set sail on the 8th with the following ships: *Hollandia, Middelburg,* the *Geunieerde Provincien, Delft, Rotterdam, Amsterdam, Hoorn, Zeelandia,* the yacht *Pauw*

---

419 About 37.5 grams.

420 This is the Yang di Pertuan Ala'udin and Raja Bongsu.

421 Where they would presumably guard, as mentioned earlier, the area around the conflucence of the Johor River with the Tebrau Strait off Changi Point and Pulau Ubin.

422 The coinage corresponds to 270 and 540 kilograms respectively.

423 Measurement in Dutch *vadem;* about 16.7 meters.

and a prize[424] that had been taken. They had the beginning of the ebb with a northeasterly wind and continued on a southeasterly course until the morning of the 11th, when they saw an unknown sail. When they approached it, they found it was a yacht named *Goede Hoop*,[425] coming straight from the fatherland, bringing news of the Twelve Years Truce and the instructions from the Directors. These they would have to follow from then on, in matters of war as well as trade, and also concerning agreements that were to be made with kings and princes.[426] The aforementioned yacht had left Banten no less than two months earlier. It was accompanied by a sloop from Zeeland and had been out of sight for seven weeks. That same day they arrived in the Palembang Strait[427] where they saw land on both sides. These shallows can be navigated freely. One will find no less water there than 5 or 6 fathoms[428] depth from the muddy clay, so that there is no risk in it, although the Portuguese maps indicate otherwise....

---

424 From the French "prise" (caught, taken); a ship that has been seized or taken by force.

425 Lit. "Good Hope".

426 For an English translation of this document dated 11 April, 1608, see CMJ, 435-40.

427 The present-day Strait of Bangka.

428 About 8.4-10 meters.

Document 9

Agreement and Remonstrance of Admiral Verhoeff and his Broad Council Submitted to the Kings of Johor

[This is a written record of the negotiations which took place between Admiral Verhoeff supported by senior officers in the broad council and the rulers of Johor in early 1609. This record reveals different understandings on the Dutch and Johorese sides of the terms and conditions laid down by treaties which Admiral Matelieff had arranged in May and September 1606. Given that Melaka had not yet been wrested from the Portuguese in the opening weeks of 1609, Admiral Verhoeff and his officers followed instructions from the Gentlemen Directors to request permission from the Johor ruler(s) to construct a fortress in Johor. As the following testimony reveals, this request was turned down. In reply thereunto, Verhoeff and his broad council drafted a petition or remonstrance that they handed to the court. It does not appear that the demands put down in this petition were ever met.][429]

Shortly after this, Admiral Verhoeff returned the [copy of the] agreement[430] that had been made between His

---

429   Netscher, *De Nederlanders in Djohor en Siak*, 20-5.

430   This refers to the second agreement between Matelieff and the rulers of Johor of 23 September 1606.

Majesty, Yang di Pertuan,[431] and Admiral Matelieff to the king of Johor, Raja Seberang. [The admiral] leaving it to [Raja Seberang] enquired if His Majesty whether wished to fulfil it. To which the reply was "Yes." The admiral replied in kind to His Majesty that he deemed the agreement valid and wanted to fulfil it, pointing out to His Majesty the clause in the second agreement made between His Majesty and Admiral Matelieff. To which His Majesty replied that that clause was void since Melaka had not been taken, and furthermore no mention of these confirmations of the Melaka articles was made in his Malay version of the agreement. As to the third article of the aforementioned contract, it states: "Since it is necessary for the Most Mighty Gentlemen States" etc.,[432] His Majesty replied that he had fulfilled and kept that article, as well as the entire contract in all its clauses, according to the Malay translation, for instance: giving locations to the Company [employees] residing in his country, as well as providing safety for people and ships in his harbors and allowing all necessary repairs.

The Lord Admiral then, in accordance with the agreement in Dutch, requested a location to build a fort or stronghold in order to resist His Majesty's and our enemies together with him. His Majesty refused this completely, because Admiral Matelieff had never requested such a thing and no mention was made of it in his Malay agreement— only of a location to build houses for the merchants and to provide roadsteads and ports for the ships to moor, both on the mainland and on the islands. The admiral asked again: since His Majesty said that he had fulfilled the agreement, would His Majesty not be willing to allow a fort to be built in his country, either far from his residence or close to it, for the defence against [their mutual] enemies? His Majesty replied that two admirals cannot command the same fleet;

---

431   Ala'udin Ri'ayat Shah III.
432   See above, p. 111.

or he and his brother Yang di Pertuan were not willing to allow it, being unable to know if it would be good or bad.

The admiral then asked His Majesty: since he was asking the Most Mighty Gentlemen States for help and assistance against his enemies—with what, in what way and with what means would one be able to help him and at his request protect him from his enemies, if he did not allow a fort to be built? His Majesty replied that the assistance he had requested had been to conquer Melaka,[433] and so far nothing had happened on that count. But that it had never been his intention to ask for help to protect his country, since they had always been able to defend themselves with their own people and resist the enemy, without the help of others. They now requested or called for help because they thought themselves weak and by the continuous war had used up their resources since requesting assistance from Admiral Heemskerck. Earlier it had not been so difficult for them, because they had still had some income; but now that the country was closed and without income or trade, they requested the help of the Dutch for this reason. They[434] added that if Admiral Verhoeff wished to help them, he should explain the realization, and also what he found so difficult in it that he abandoned everything.

The admiral then stated that he had come [to Johor] solely with the intention to construct a fort, so that [the king's] lands and ports would be the freer and safer. [They would] thus attract all the trade and flourish from all sides, like Patani and Aceh, and make big profits. But if His Majesty desired a different kind of help, he was willing to hear his

433 This request had been made by the Johor embassy to the Dutch Republic which departed for Europe with the fleet of Admiral Jacob van Heemskerck in 1603 and returned to Johor with the fleet of Admiral Matelieff in 1605.

434 This appears to refer to the Yang di Pertuan Ala'udin and Raja Seberang (alias Raja Bongsu).

request and intention, to deliberate whether it would contribute to making the country safe and furthering trade; then he would think about it.

To this, Yang di Pertuan replied that he was not inclined to allow any forts for foreign nations, because he was willing to settle for less trade than the kings of Banten or Patani. A fort, moreover, required many things, and guarding it would take much cost and effort—costs which [Raja Bongsu] deemed superfluous, and all the more so because Holland was so far away and [the Dutch] now had their city of Banten[435] a location where they could securely wait for their enemy and resist him. He only wanted help from the admiral in the form of money and ammunition, in such quantities as the admiral, being a man experienced in war, would find to be necessary.

The admiral repeatedly asked His Majesty to state a demand, but he refused, saying only that the admiral was well able to consider what [the Johoreese] needed. [He] asked [the admiral] to realize their need, which was known now, and give it the highest priority. [Raja Bongsu] was sad about the misunderstanding which had risen from the [Malay] translation of the agreement, since it would be announced to the Most Mighty Gentlemen States that they were to have a fort in his country, which he had never intended.

Abraham van den Broeck said to this that in His Majesty's presence, he had heard the interpreter being instructed to present it this way, in accordance with the agreement written in Dutch. [Raja Bongsu] wished a copy of the Malay translation to be sent to Holland, so that it could be seen that he was not to blame.

Subsequently the following was submitted:

Remonstrance from Admiral Verhoeff, the Vice-Admiral and the Broad Council, in the name of the

---

435   Netscher erroneously reads here: Batavia.

Overleaf: Market stall in the East Indies, ascribed to A. Eckhout, 1640-1666. Rijksmuseum Amsterdam, SK-A-4070.

Gentlemen States General of the United Provinces of the Netherlands, His Princely Excellency and the Gentlemen Directors of the East India Company, to the king of Johor.

As the Lord Admiral Verhoeff has presented to his Broad Council the proposition and remonstrance made by the Lord Vice-Admiral and some members of his Broad Council to His Majesty at Batu Sawar, as well as the reply to it, from which it can be understood that His Majesty in no way intends to allow us a fort in his country for the defence of His Majesty's subjects and ours and to attack our common enemies, which was entirely contrary to the intention of the aforementioned Council, having explicit orders from the Most Mighty Gentlemen States General, His Princely Excellency and their own masters to build a fort, in which they understand His Majesty's and our entire prosperity to reside—it has been decided: to present to His Majesty once more the difficulties which could arise from this, to see that His Majesty, being thus forewarned, be persuaded to enter into a reasonable agreement with us.

First, since it is well-known that the Portuguese in all likelihood will come upon His Majesty here within four months' time with huge numbers of men, and we do not yet see sufficient locations where His Majesty could stave them off, His Majesty and his subjects as well as we and the goods and cargoes that we leave here are in great danger and have to expect utter destruction, unless His Majesty were to grant the request.

Regarding His Majesty's objection that our men might be interested in their women, goods or otherwise, after the manner of the Portuguese, we are offering to make such an agreement as will satisfy His Majesty completely, by which any insolence will be averted.

As to His Majesty's claim that two admirals cannot command the same fleet, may it please His Majesty to understand that it is not our intention to interfere with his authority, but on the contrary to recognize him in every way as sovereign of his country, and that we would content ourselves with a captain to command the fort; and he would take an oath of loyalty to His Majesty as well as to the Most Mighty Gentlemen States.

If His Majesty granted our request, we could leave some ships here to guard against the enemies, to protect the friends and to let His Majesty have a share of any size on which we could agree with one another, in any spoils that might be taken. By which His Majesty should expect trade and prosperity in his lands, apart from the fact that if His Majesty is in trouble with sieges, we would have to assist him with financial means, just like otherwise in such a case. We would leave a cargo of pieces of cloth from the Coromandel Coast and Bengal in store here, with which the surrounding lands could also be supplied, looking for trade and attracting it here in the same way as otherwise and hindering the trade to Melaka as much as possible with our ships. From this His Majesty can expect not a little profit. We hope that His Majesty after ample consideration of this remonstrance will easily understand that it is greatly to his benefit."

The sultan of Johor and Raja Abd'ullah[436] merely replied "that the kings were presently in great distress and had fallen to that state because of the alliance made with the Dutch, and because of it they ran the risk of going down; in part because now, without assistance in the form of money and ammunition, warfare and ships, they were unable to resist their and our enemies."

This reply occasioned the following deliberation and resolution in the broad council of Verhoeff's fleet:

> One has certain knowledge that the King, Yang di Pertuan, has sought to make some profitable agreement with the Portuguese upon the Lord Admiral Matelieff's departure, which would have been to the direct disadvantage of the Most Mighty Gentlemen States and the Directors. This is apparent from the original sent to the Gentlemen Directors by the Lord Admiral Matelieff, of which Admiral Verhoeff has seen a copy. Taking into account, moreover that, if we did not assist (in accordance with the request) the kings in fortifying and building their city, they could become unfavourably inclined towards us; the more so since we are not paying any customs, tolls, anchorage tolls, weighing fees for merchandise etc. Consequently the kings have little or no profit from us and from our residing here and have therefore in fairness declined the request, and might leave us and choose a more advantageous party for the sake of their subjects, who have fallen into misery through the war. We would have reason to fear therefore that not only this place and this kingdom could in all likelihood desert us at any time, but those of Patani and Banten as well. Considering the above, it has been jointly decided by the Lord Admiral, Vice-Admiral and the Broad Council,

---

436   That is the proper name of Raja Bongsu or Raja Seberang.

firstly, that we shall assist the aforementioned kings with a sum of money as well as two ships that shall be left at the mouth of or near their river[437] (namely the ship *De Leeuw met Pijlen*[438] and the yacht *De Griffioen*[439]), for the protection of Their Majesties' subjects against the enemies—otherwise [these enemies] would have free access to the kings' ports just as their friends do. [The two ships stationed in the Johor River shall also] attack the enemies coming from Macao, China and some other places.[440] These ships, their commanding officers and the men will follow the instructions of the Lord Admiral, Vice-Admiral and the Broad Council, who will deliberate on the matter and arrange everything.

In return we request and insist on the concept of the agreement hereafter, which if we do not obtain, the above resolution will be subject to reconsideration.

First, that the kings will not enter into any negotiations with the Portuguese or others, our enemies, regarding peace, truce or otherwise, without our advice. We shall do likewise and involve the aforementioned kings in all our agreements.

That the kings—since they are going to live up in the new city[441] with their people and we will thus

---

437 That is, the Johor River.

438 Lit. "The Lion with Arrows."

439 Lit. "The Griffin."

440 The enemies here are the Portuguese.

441 A new city was being constructed at the time of Verhoeff's visit. The admiral and his officers had been taken there by boat on an inspection tour. The new city under construction is believed to have been Pasar (sometimes Pasir) Raja, located further up the Johor River. See also RWME, 441, and document 8.

be without people around our lodgings, making it dangerous to stay there and risk the cargo—will grant us, at a location of our choice, sufficient space to build a house of wood and stone as big as necessary, and allow us to build it to keep ourselves safe.

That it please the kings to allow us free trade in all their lands, without prohibiting or stopping it at any time.

That the pepper coming to their lands may be received by us pure and clear, without [needing to] supply bags for the pepper.

That we may use our own weights, measures and steelyards when receiving and supplying goods.

That Their Majesties will provide us with letters of recommendation to their subjects and neighbours so that we may enjoy the benefit and the pre-eminence which their families and subjects have.

That it please the kings to grant us, as they have thus far, freedom from tolls, customs, anchorage fees and all other taxes and levies throughout their lands.

That His Majesty assist us in collecting the debts that his subjects as well as foreign nations owe us. [This mostly concerns] the Chinese trade, which cannot be done unless one pays by cash in advance. Then if [the Chinese] want to cheat us and keep the money, our people will try to obtain payment or recompensation from among the Chinese junks arriving [during the] next [trading season], according to Chinese law. [This is] on the condition that they [surrender to] them the bonds of the persons who have kept the money. [With these bonds] they can obtain their payment in China—since they intended to make the trade profitable to His Majesty.

Document 10

Letter by King Ala'udin of Johor
and Raja Bongsu
to Stadholder Prince Maurice of Nassau
and the Dutch States General
dated 6 February, 1609

[Coinciding with the end of Ramadan and the celebration
of Eid al-Fitr, Admiral Verhoeff arrived at the Batu Sawar
court in January 1609 to come to an agreement with Ala'udin
and Raja Bongsu. Batu Sawar had suffered a crippling blockade imposed on the Johor River by the Portuguese in 1608
and the Johorese were clearly disappointed by the apparent
unwillingness of the Dutch to engage their common enemy
in battle. A request to wage war against Patani instead was
put on the table by the Johor rulers, but to no avail. In turn,
Verhoeff's request to tighten the alliance and modify existing arrangements anchored in the 1606 Johor-VOC treaties
was turned down (see documents 8 and 9). The present letter dated 6 February, 1609, was passed to Admiral Verhoeff
when he raised anchor and set sail from the waters off Johor
Lama. Although it mirrors a sense of disappointment on the
part of the Johor rulers, the letter reveals two very important things: first, the initiative for forging diplomatic relations
via the ambassador Megat Mansur in 1603 had clearly been a
Johorese initiative. Second, in petitioning Stadholder Prince
Maurice and the States General for military assistance against
Patani, the origins of Johor's (dynastic) conflict with Patani

Left: Painted portrait of Stadholder Maurice of Nassau, the Prince of Orange, by M.J. van Mierevelt, c. 1613-1620. Rijksmuseum Amsterdam, SK-A-255-00

are explained in some detail.]

In the name of God, Lord of everything that was created in the world, and of the Prophet Muhammad, called and sent in His name. This letter is from Yang di Pertuan, King of Johor and Melaka, and from Raja Seberang, brother to Yang di Pertuan, who keep a firm and eternal friendship with the Most Mighty Gentlemen of the States General and His Princely Excellency, as well as with the admirals and captains who come and are here, who by their wisdom protect Yang di Pertuan's city and lands. Sending this letter to the Most Mighty Gentlemen of the States General and His Princely Excellency in Holland, judges on land and sea and over the entire might of the United Provinces, which they have in their power, and none is found who can resist and expel them. The kings who have suffered damage from their enemies and have been betrayed shall be helped when they tell of their distress, if they so desire or ask; so that their names are most extolled and praised: we also expect help, requesting it of the aforesaid Gentlemen.

As regards the dishonor or shame inflicted on us by the people of Melaka: there is a place or city[442] named Patani, better populated than we are, against which we have no power to avenge the shame inflicted on us. For when we wrote to our brother in Holland,[443] we did not expound everything in that letter, lest it be known to many. But by word of mouth we charged a man with it, a powerful man

---

442 This settlement or city is most likely to be understood in the sense of the Malay negeri.

443 That is to the "King of Holland". See the glossary *(King of Holland)*.

who was our kin and whom we sent to Holland to the Most Mighty Gentlemen of the States and His Princely Excellency, our brother, as an ambassador, in the company of Admiral Jacob Heemskerck. His name was Megat Mansur. He did not reach our brother, because he died at sea; the ones who were left and reached Holland were only slaves. So when Admiral Pieter Willemsz. Verhoeff reached Melaka and, from there, Johor, we talked with him and together concluded that the fleet brought by the Admiral and our forces were unable to conquer Melaka for the time being. We were no longer able to stop ourselves and had to explain the dishonor and shame inflicted on us, and asked him to conquer the city of Patani for us.[444] The Admiral with his [broad] council decided on this matter and replied to us that he dared not undertake it, being afraid to enter upon such a thing, because he had not been sent by the Most Mighty Gentlemen States for that purpose but only to conquer Melaka or the Malukus. The admiral told us that, if we wanted to take the city with his help, we should write as much to the Gentlemen States and His Princely Excellency,[445] our brother. If he gave his permission, a few Admirals would conquer it with little effort.

It is because of this matter that we write to the Most Mighty Gentlemen States and His Princely Excellency, our brother, requesting some help in order to lay down the disgrace brought upon us. Furthermore it is our feeling and the sincere opinion of our heart that, if that city is conquered, the power of the Gentlemen States and His Princely Excellency, our brother, will be much increased, even more than by conquering Melaka; in part because all other places could then see and notice our brother's just and powerful help to us, who are now at the end of our might and means.

Now, if the Gentlemen States and His Princely Excellency, our brother, with sincere hearts and love want to

---

444   See p. 35 above.

445   Stadholder Prince Maurice of Nassau.

come to our aid with a few ships to be sent here, we request that a letter to that effect be addressed to us: to help us as we ask, with full power, in the name of the Gentlemen States and His Princely Excellency, our brother, so that all the surrounding lands may know, both there and here, that our brother wishes to support and elevate us by his help.

We will furthermore tell of Admiral Pieter Willemsz. Verhoeff's request upon his arrival in our city and country, when he asked for a place to build a fort. To which we replied only with Cornelis Matelieff de Jonge's agreement made at that time, translated or interpreted by Lodewijck Isaacsz., which the admiral demanded of us, but which did not mention giving any places to build forts, only land to build houses or conduct trade, or some islands to repair ships, as well as mooring places for ships, in the city as well as on our islands. Admiral Pieter Willemsz. Verhoeff had a copy of that agreement made to be sent to Holland and shown to the Most Mighty Gentlemen States and His Princely Excellency. We also request that no further changes be made to the agreement concluded between us and Admiral Cornelis Matelieff de Jonge, and we will follow and keep it for a very long time. We request that any admirals coming from Holland do not make any other agreement than that one. If the city of Patani is conquered, which inflicted the dishonor upon us, then some agreement could be made in addition to the agreement of Melaka made with Admiral Matelieff.

We would greatly desire that the Noble Gentlemen States and His Princely Excellency, our brother, avenge the dishonor done to us, which was this: First we were six brothers. When the king of Patani heard this, he asked for our eldest brother to be married to his daughter; our father consented and he was sent there with some of our younger brothers to be in his company there. Having been there for a long time, our younger brother violated our eldest brother's housewife, whom he had married there. For this, our younger brother was killed by the eldest. Then our eldest brother also killed his own housewife, daughter to the king[446] of Patani, because of the crime she had committed with our youngest brother. Over this, the king of Patani, the father, also took our eldest brother's life, for no other reason than that our eldest brother had wanted to erase the dishonor done to him and us. As we understand it, if our younger brother had not made such a gross mistake with our eldest brother's housewife, he would have been brought to death unjustly. After our eldest brother had taken note of the matter, he rightly killed the youngest. For which the king of Patani has had our eldest brother brought to death as well— and this is the shame and dishonor which was done to us and which we bring to the Most Mighty Gentlemen States and His Princely Excellency, our brother. For in this land, all the laws and customs are that if a woman misbehaves, the partner or lover is killed in the same way. This is, we say, the dishonor done to us: that over a just case of law of our eldest brother against the youngest, the king of Patani then had the eldest brought to death so unjustly. We request that this be avenged by your help and that our disgrace and shame may thus be erased before all kings, both there with you and here.

---

446   Read: queen. If the term "Raja Patani" had featured in the Malay original of this letter, the gender of that ruler would not be necessarily known to the translator, and he might have simply assumed it to refer to a king.

Document 11

Letter of King Ala'udin of Johor
and Raja Bongsu
to Stadholder Prince Maurice of Nassau,
dated 8 December, 1609

[This letter to Stadholder Prince Maurice was written on learning that the Dutch Republic had entered into a truce with the king of Spain and Portugal. It reveals that the Johor rulers were disappointed by the Dutch. This letter is important and informative as it shows that Johor understood itself as an equal treaty partner with the Dutch, that the rulers had no reservations to voice their disappointment in a formal letter of complaint, and that they wanted to take up matters directly with the responsible persons in Europe.]

The mighty king of Johor, lord of all the surrounding places and islands, and Raja di Ilir or Bongsu, his brother of equal descent, steadfast in all his doings, to Maurice of Orange, count of Nassau and Catzenellenbogen, Vianen, Dietz and Meurs, marquis of Veere and Vlissingen, governor of the duchy of Guelders and the counties of Holland and Zeeland, Zutphen and the seigniory of East-Friesland, of Utrecht and Overijssel and admiral and captain-general at sea, this letter serves to say that we received His Princely Excellency's previous letter with great joy and understood its contents well, since our brother's good affection toward us is being continued according to our alliance and our hope is in nothing but in our brother, who has the power to return Melaka to us. But at first it inwardly saddened us very much to hear that our brother has made some agreement with the king of Portugal, for in whom shall we now place our hope to regain the city of Melaka, if this agreement with the king of Portugal proceeds? Therefore, if there is any friendship and affection left toward us, we kindly suggest that one should first help us to recover Melaka, so that the name of our brother may be honored and spread over the entire world. In this matter we still place our only hope and trust in our brother.

Furthermore, a request is made in our brother's letter to expand or renew our previous alliance. But what purpose is there to this continuous changing and renewing? It would therefore be our desire that our brother may sometime send a person of distinction here with full power and authority, so that an indissoluble agreement may be made with that person, which will last until Judgment Day. Even if 20 or 30 admirals came then, no changes could be made to it. For as it is now, an admiral comes, we make a good agreement with him, and then another comes and changes it. In this way there will be no end to making agreements. But if it could be done as we have described here, then there would be an end to the contract-making and there would be no one who could change them anymore.

[Sealed with the seal of Raja di Ilir or Bongsu.]

Document 12

Johannes Verken
Description of Raja Bongsu of Johor,
January or February 1609

[Johannes Verken was a native of Meissen in Saxony (now Germany) and a member of Admiral Verhoeff's crew. The larger ships belonging to the fleet lay at anchor around Johor Lama while smaller craft brought the admiral and some of his officers to the capital Batu Sawar for discussions with King Ala'udin and Raja Bongsu. Verken, however, remained at Johor Lama. His diary was first published in German as part of Theodor de Bry's travel series and can be found in the *Neundter Theil der Orientalischen Indien* (Ninth Voyage [of the Dutch] to the East Indies) of 1612. The following excerpt recounts Verkens's personal description of Raja Bongsu of Johor.][447]

... With reference to the king of Johor, who is also known as Raja Bongsu, he is still a young man in his 30s. When he came aboard our ship, he was wearing a white cot-

---

447 Johannes Verken, "Molukkenreise, 1607-1612," in *Reisebeschreibungen von Deutschen Beamten und Kriegsleuten im Dienst der Niederländisch West- und Ost-Indischen Kompanien, 1602-1797*, ed. S.P. l'Honoré Naber, II (The Hague: Martinus Nijhoff, 1930), 58-9. Another English translation of this passage is found in GPFT, 258-9.

ADMIRAL MATELIEFF'S SINGAPORE AND JOHOR (1606-1616)

ton shirt that reached down to knee level. Around his body he wore a beautifully colored, striped cotton cloth, which reached halfway down to his feet. Otherwise, he was bare on his body and legs. But he wore on his feet a pair of black velvet slippers, and around his head he had wrapped a black headpiece of silk. Around his neck he wore three golden chains, which were completely inlaid with gemstones. Around his left arm he wore two thick golden rings, and around his right arm [another] one. On his fingers he wore six precious rings. He also had a dagger at his side which was made in a very extraordinary manner, and which [the Malays] call a kris. The handle and the blade were made of pure, clear wrought gold and were studded with diamonds, rubies and sapphires in such a way that the same dagger was estimated by the Dutch to have a value of more than 50,000 guilders.[448] [Raja Bongsu] was in his appearance and body a well-proportioned person, rather tall, articulate, and fair-skinned both on his face and body.

---

448   This sum was equivalent to about 535 kilograms of coin-grade silver.

Glossary

Amar di Raja This term is found in the printed version of the *Journal* as *Agi di Raja*. It is uncertain and may very well represent a corruption of the Malay title *Sri Amar di Raja* (sometimes also spelled *Diraja*). According to the study of the Melaka sultanate by Muhammad Yusof Hashim, this was the title held by the *perdana mentri*, the third highest official in the Melaka sultanate in order of precedence following the bendahara (chief minister) and the *penghulu bendahari* (treasurer). Sri Amar di Raja was a member of the royal family. As a successor polity of Melaka, the Johor sultanate had retained most of the important Malay titles and their order of precedence. See also the separate entry for bendahara.[449]

bendahara (Also: *bendara*). A high-ranking, hereditary position in a Malay polity who in more recent times has become synonymous to the "chief minister" and "minister of interior". He came first in precedence after the ruler (*shah, sultan*). According to the *Undang-undang Melaka* (Laws of Melaka), a legal code that retained authority in Malay polities throughout most of the early modern period, the bendahara was

---

449 Muhammad Yusof Hashim, *The Malay Sultanate of Malacca*, 109, 112.

specifically given "jurisdiction for instance[s] over those who are holding office, and those who rank as *tuan* [lord] or *sida* (court officers) and the children of high dignitaries." The bendahara importantly also served as the master of ceremonies (such as the *sirih nobat* ceremony, that is the serving of betel and playing of the royal orchestra in the presence of the bendahara). He legitimised activities at the court through ritual. The bendahara also received gifts from foreign traders coming to Melaka as well as from emissaries of foreign rulers. Tomé Pires called him a "kind of chief-justice in all civil and criminal affairs". The bendahara "also has charge of the king's revenue. He can order any person to be put to death, of whatsoever rank and condition, whether nobleman or foreigner; but first of all he informs the king, and both decide the matter in consultation with the [laksamana] and the [temenggong]". In Portuguese Melaka, the bendahara evolved into a representative of the non-Christian, non-Muslim communities of Melaka (such as notably the Hindus and Buddhists), while his counterpart, the temenggong became the representative of the Muslims. In late 16th and early 17th century Johor, the bendahara was together with the laksamana one of the most important "merchants" or "merchant-officials."[450]

bezoar (Portuguese: *piedras de bazares, beçares*; Malay: *guliga*) Bezoars are concrements found in different parts of the intestinal tracts of mammals, especially in ruminants. When

450 CMJ, 461-2; GLA I, 115-6; GVOC, 18; HJ, 84; JCSJ, 97-8; JDC, 305-6; PSM, 155, 178-9, 203-13, 338; SMS, 334, UUM, 62-3; Muhammad Yusof Hashim, *The Malay Sultanate of Malacca*, 28-34, Pires, *Suma Oriental*, II, 264.

harvested from monkeys (so-called "monkey stones"), the bezoars represent gallstones found in apes. Bezoars are not exactly the most sightly, but their potential value as a life-saving medication and their deployment as a panacea in almost all medication in Europe during the early modern period rendered the price of bezoars more costly than diamonds. In the traditional cultures of Arabia, Europe, India, and the Indianized cultures of Southeast Asia, bezoars were also believed to possess magical or mystical properties to ward off wicked spells and many forms of evil. For this reason, they were also mounted in jewelry and headpieces of royalty or religious leaders. Among the most expensive of all were the porcupine bezoars which were harvested on the Malay Peninsula, Sumatra, the Riau Archipelago and on Borneo. Johor (specifically its capital Batu Sawar), Siak, Pahang, Sambas, Sukadana, Banjarmasin and Brunei Bay were among the most important trading centers of this rare and very costly product. Porcupine bezoars were widely considered the sovereign remedy against cholera, dysentery and other life-threatening diseases and also against poisoning. In the early modern period, bezoars were often treated like precious stones. They were sold by the carat, and the price per carat rose exponentially, just as is the case with diamonds and other known (cut or polished) gems. For this reason—and especially because of the bezoar's alleged life-saving properties—jewellers generally dealt in these "stones" on behalf of their wealthy clients. See the illustration on p. 63.[451]

---

451   BOC, I.1, 728; BOC, III, 587; CMJ, 463-4; EFS, II, 1395; GLA, I, 107-9; GVOC, 20, 89; HJ, 90-1; JCSJ, 98; JDC, 307-8; Borschberg, *The Trade, Forgery and Medicinal Use of Porcupine Be-*

camphor   (Arabic: *kafur*; Malay: *kapur*). In the early modern period, there were fundamentally two types of camphor traded: natural tropical camphor (sometimes also called "Barus camphor" or "edible camphor") and synthetically produced Japanese laurel camphor. The latter could be applied externally (i.e., on the skin) to treat bites and certain skin disorders. It was cheap and plentifully produced in China. By contrast, tropical camphor from Borneo or Sumatra was not toxic when ingested and was widely deployed in Asian as well as European medicine during the early modern period. Tropical camphor was most commonly used to purge intestinal parasites. The Arabs and Indians (mainly Gujaratis) chiefly procured their tropical camphor at the ports of Barus or Pariaman located on the western coast of Sumatra (at the time these ports were controlled by the Acehnese). The Chinese, however, purchased their supplies from Borneo. Jan Huyghen van Linschoten claimed that the camphor from Borneo was the best in all of Asia. Of the camphor tree, Manuel Godinho de Erédia wrote: "... it is a tall stout tree, and the camphor-liquor flows from the holes in the bark. The scented wood is much used in the carpenter's craft, for beds and tables of superior grade." See the illustration on p. 63.[452]

clove   (Dutch: *kruidnagel*; Malay: *cengkeh*). Cloves are, strictly speaking, the aromatic flower buds of the *Eugenia aromatica*. In the period under review

---

zoars, 60-78; Borschberg, "The Euro-Asian Trade in Bezoar Stones (approx. 1500-1700)," in *Artistic and Cultural Exchanges between Europe and Asia, 1400-1900: Rethinking Markets, Workshops and Collections*, ed. M. North (Aldershot: Ashgate, 2010), 29-43.

452   CMJ, 465; EFS, II, 1396; JDC, 311; MGED, 26.

as well as for the early modern era as a whole, the Maluku Island group, specifically the islands of Ternate, Tidore, Moti, Makian, and Bacan (in addition to a few other minor islands) were the only places where clove trees grew. While Jan Huyghen van Linschoten had extolled that the Malukus have "so many cloves you can fill the world" with them, total production on all the Maluku Islands during the first decade of the 17th century was estimated by John Saris at 3,975 Maluku *bahar* or about 1,085.6 metric tons. The breakdown of the harvest on the principal Maluku islands was appraised by Saris as follows: Makian: 1,090 bahar; Ternate: 1,000 Maluku bahar; Tidore: 900 bahar; Moti: 600 bahar; Bacan: 300 bahar; Meau (Maju): 50 bahar; and "Batta China": 35 bahar. By contrast, Matelieff appraised aggregate production a few years later (c. 1615) at less than half that amount, namely 1,500 Maluku bahar or about 409.65 metric tons. The decline in production and harvesting at the turn of the 16th and 17th centuries has been linked to the wars and civil strife in and around the Maluku region. Some reports claim that there were no people to take in the harvest and that the cloves were rotting on the ground. At a cash price of 50 reals-of-eight per Maluku bahar, the total production figures cited by Saris and Matelieff amount to a market value of 5.43 and 2.03 metric tons respectively of coin-grade silver. Like all spices in this period, cloves were (and still are) believed to bear certain pharmacological properties that include cleansing of the kidney and liver and strengthening of the heart. Cloves were also used against colds and headaches, as a breath freshener and famously also as an aphrodisiac.[453]

---

453   CMJ, 469; Satow, *The Voyage of Captain John Saris to Japan*,

factor, factory   Resident head of a so-called factory (sometimes called "lodge" or "house" in VOC sources). The term is of Italian or also Portuguese origin and in earliest times referred to a commercial agent or the head of a collection and billing station. In the context of East Indian trade however, the feitoria or "factory" was often a heavily fortified structure with a resident population rendering support services to the factory and its broader activities. These settlements were usually beyond, or specifically exempted from, the jurisdiction of the local Asian overlord by treaty. The factor was in charge of the entire operations within a given compound and in the case of larger settlements, also oversaw public works.[454]

Gentlemen   (Also: *Gentlemen XVII*, a lit. translation
Directors   of the Dutch *Heren XVII*). The expression "Gentlemen Directors" refers to the central board of 17 directors of the VOC. The board drew members from all six chambers of the company according to their relative size and capitalization. Amsterdam had the largest number of directors, followed by Middelburg. Collectively the Gentlemen XVII represented the highest decision-making body of the VOC.[455]

King of Holland This is a term coined in the early years of the VOC to refer to the States General and sometimes also the Stadholder(s) of the Dutch

---

58–9; David Bulbeck, Anthony Reid, Lay Cheng Tan and Wu Yiqi, ed., *Southeast Asian Exports since the 14th Century: Cloves, Pepper, Coffee and Sugar* (Singapore: ISEAS, 1998), 17–59, esp. 34–5.

454   CMJ, 476; GVOC, 42; HJ, 345-7; JDC, 320-1.

455   CMJ, 541-2.

Republic. It appears to have been employed by rulers and peoples of the Malay Archipelago who found it impossible to imagine a country without a king or ruler, since the absence of a raja was tantamount to disorder and chaos. A people that had deposed its ruler (as indeed the Dutch had done via the Act of Abjuration in 1581) would have committed *derhaka* (treason)—a very grave and unforgivable sin in Malay culture—and would have therefore openly challenged their hereditary ruler's mystical right or divine mandate to rule (*daulat*). Rulers and peoples of the Malay Archipelago would have found it equally challenging—if not impossible—to grasp the European idea of a republican federation along the lines of the Dutch Republic or the Swiss Confederation (*Eidgenossenschaft*). From the late 16th to the late 18th century, the northern Netherlands had come to assume (by default, it should be added here) a republican form of government. Technically Holland was only one of seven provinces of the federation, but without doubt, it was the most significant and home not only to major trading cities, but also to all but one of the chambers of the VOC (the exception being Middelburg in the province of Zeeland).[456]

mace   (Malay: *bunga pala*; Dutch: *foelie, macis* and other variants; German: *Muskatblüte*). A layer of skin separating the flesh of the fruit of *Myristica fragrans* ("nutmeg tree") from its kernel. The nutmeg tree is native to the Banda Islands in present-day Indonesia and in the early modern period grew only there. Mace has a slightly different flavor from nutmeg and

---

456   CMJ, 488-9.

for this reason is marketed as a separate spice. It was used in cosmetics and in medicine as a stimulant and aphrodisiac. The Portuguese medic Garcia da Orta reported that the price of mace was three times higher than for nutmeg. See also the separate entries for *nutmeg* and *Banda*.[457]

mandarin   This is generally believed to be a European corruption of the Sanskrit-derived term *mantrin* (minister, advisor). Although the title *mantri* (or *menteri*) is also widely employed in Malay, the specific term mandarin is most often associated today with officials of a Confucian state. Hobson-Jobson rightly observed that the term was applied indiscriminately by the Portuguese to all sorts of officials across Asia on account of the term's etymological resemblance to the Portuguese verb *mandar* (to govern).[458]

nutmeg   (Malay: *buah pala*; Dutch: *nooten, nootmuskaat*; German: *Muskatnuß*, lit. the nut from Muscat). Nutmeg and mace are separate spices gained from the fruit of the *Myristica fragrans* (nutmeg tree). Nutmeg is the fruit kernel's inner core. The tree is native to the Banda Islands and in the 16th and 17th centuries grew only there, though some reports of the late 16th century mention nutmeg cultivation on the island of Ceylon. Total production of nutmeg would have been smaller than the aggregate size (and value) of the clove harvest on the nearby Maluku Islands. For this reason, Matelieff thought it both possible and feasible to "get all the nutmeg and mace into our hands", that is to create a Dutch monopoly in this spice. He advised: "… above all, we should get the land of

---

457   CMJ, 493-4; GLA, II, 1-2; GVOC, 70.
458   CMJ, 495; GLA, II, 20-2; JDC, 328-9.

Banda under the Gentlemen States [General's] authority and ensure it for ourselves in the manner I have explained previously, the sooner the better, or news of it will reach the Spaniards or the English and then it will be too late." Like all spices, nutmeg was (and still is) believed to possess certain pharmacological properties. In the early modern period it was used to strengthen the mind and the heart, warm the stomach, cleanse the liver, facilitate passing of urine and stool, and as a remedy for stomach wind. See also the separate entries for *clove*, *mace*, and *Maluku*.[459]

orang kaya (Also: *arangkaio*, *orangcay* and other spellings). A Malay term that literally translates into "wealthy person". In certain parts of the Malay Archipelago, the expression, however, does not refer so much to wealth as to power. An orang kaya is also a person of authority and good standing, and the term is also used as a title. Moreland described the expression as a "general title for persons of high position", here a reference in relation to their status at the courts of the Malay sultans. Blagden further elucidated that orang kaya is the "title of ministers of state, vassals or tributary chiefs, court officials, etc."[460]

orang laut (Also: sea nomad; sea gypsy). The Portuguese and Spanish name commonly used is *selates* or *saletes*, the former of which is rooted in the Malay word *selat* meaning "strait". Thus the *selates* are the people who live in or around the selat or strait. In English, the term "sea gypsy" was used in the past, but is now considered

---

459 CMJ, 498-9.
460 CMJ, 500; BOC, II.3, 613; EFS, II, 1406; GVOC, 83; HJ, 644–5; JDC, 331.

a pejorative. *Orang laut* translates from the Malay language as "people of the sea". In precolonial times, the *orang laut* were loyal to the Melaka sultan, but later they paid allegiance to the sultan of Johor, at least until the end of the Melaka dynasty toward the end of the 17th century. They often acted as the sultan's navy, patrolled the Straits and acted as paid pilots to passing European, Chinese and Arab vessels. The Portuguese chronicler João de Barros claimed that the *selates* "lived afloat rather than on land. Their sons were born and bred on the sea and had no fixed bases ashore."[461]

Paduka Raja A Malay titular prefix for the bendahara deriving from the Sanskrit *pāduka* (slipper, shoe), which according to Blagden "refer[s] to the exalted position of the titulary, whose slippers were treated higher than the head of the humble suppliant addressing him." The title suggests that the office bearer could speak to the shoe or slipper, but not look up to, or face, the ruler directly. In later colonial times European governors titled themselves in Malay as *Paduka Sahabat Beta* (lit. shoe friend of the sultan).[462]

pepper (Malay: *lada hitam*; Latin: *Piper nigrum*). The fruit of a creeping vine (*Piperaceae*) that is thought to have originated in India and was transplanted to Southeast Asia before the arrival of the Europeans in the early modern period.

---

461 CMJ, 500; BOC, II.3, 613; EFS, II, 1406; GVOC, 83; HJ, 644-5; JCSJ, 104; JDC, 336-7; SMS, 335-6; David E. Sopher, *The Sea Nomads, a Study Based on Literature of the Maritime Boat People of Southeast Asia* (Singapore: Lim Bian Han, 1965); Oliver W. Wolters, *Early Indonesian Commerce: A Study of the Origins of Srivijaya* (Ithaca: Cornell University Press, 1967), 222 (citing Barros).

462 CMJ, 501.

Like all spices, pepper was, and still is, believed
to possess certain medicinal properties. In
the early modern period, it was used to help
eyesight, reduce swelling, cure toothaches
and headaches, and as a remedy against
cholera. Pepper has also been mentioned as an
ingredient for dart poison among the Dayaks
of Borneo. Pepper was once extensively used
for conserving foods. Today it is chiefly used
as a stimulant and in detoxification. Unlike
the other classic spices from the Indonesian
Archipelago (nutmeg, mace and cloves), pepper
production had not declined at the turn of the
16th and 17th centuries. On the contrary, the
size of the harvest had doubled over the course
of about one and a half decades between 1595
and 1610. The Portuguese medic Garcia da Orta
underscored that most pepper was exported to
China, Martaban, Pegu, Arabia and the Red
Sea region and added "much will be taken
westward by the Moors".[463] See the illustration
on p. 59.

Raja Bongsu A Malay title meaning the "Young" or "Junior
King"; *bongsu* being an endearing term in Malay
referring to the youngest son. Raja Bongsu, who
himself was to rule as sultan of Johor between
1613/5 and 1623 as Abdullah Ma'ayat Shah,
was also variously known as Raja Seberang
and Raja di Ilir. At the time of Matelieff's
seaborne attack on Portuguese Melaka and
later during his visit to the Batu Sawar court,
political power in Johor appears to have been
multipolar, and effectively divided between the
four surviving sons of Raja Ali Jalla bin Abdul
Jalil. This division of power is said to have been

---

463 CMJ, 503-4; Bulbeck, Reid, Lay and Wu, ed., *Southeast Asian Exports since the 14th Century*, 60–106.

engineered by the bendahara, Paduka Raja, Tun Sri Lanang. Although Ala'udin formally held the title of sultan, many of the affairs of state— including especially foreign relations (and that would include waging war) was apparently the purview of Raja Bongsu. As is further evident from the writings of Matelieff, Raja Bongsu had an *istana* (palace, residence) and vassals at Kota Seberang, a settlement located across the river and slightly downstream from Batu Sawar. W.G. Shellabear has identified the location as Pengkalan Lama. In addition to Kota Seberang, Raja Bongsu is also said to have had a personal dependency in Sambas on the great island of Borneo. Various issues concerning the genealogy of Raja Bongsu have been historicised and problematized, among others, by Cheah Boon Kheng and Paulo Pinto.[464]

Raja Lela   (Also *Raja Lela Wangsa*). A title of nobility, used in the Acehnese context, and expressly mentioned in the *Bustan-as-Salatin* (Garden of Kings) to describe a person who is intimately involved with or related to the royal family. It was also used in connection with the Buginese in Aceh, such as for example in the instance

---

464   CMJ, 507-8; JCSJ, 105-6; JDC, 337; PSM, 238-55; P.G. Leupe, "The Siege and Capture of Malacca from the Portuguese in 1640-1641. Extracts from the Archives of the Dutch East India Company," trans. Mac Hacobian, *JMBRAS*, 14.1 (1936): 149. See also Cheah Boon Kheng and Peter Borschberg, "Raja Bongsu and *Sejarah Melayu* (The Malay Annals): An 'ill-starred prince' of Johor with a tragic fate (b.1571- d.1623)," forthcoming in *JMBRAS*, 2016; and W.G. Shellabear, *Sejarah Melayu* [The Malay Annals], 9th edn. (Singapore: Malaya Publishing House, 1961), 323: "... Raja 'Abdullah beristana diseberang Pengkalan Raya, maka disebut orang Raja Seberang" (Raja 'Abdullah whose palace was across the river in Pengkalan Raya, is called by others Raja Seberang).

of Ala'udin Ahmad Shah (early 18th century). The term Lela further seems to indicate a title linked to military prowess. The second part of the title, *Wangsa*, appears to be a derivative of the Sanskrit word *vamśa* (breed, race, descent). Matelieff listed a "Raja Lela" in his *Journal*, and this may very well represent a Johorese equivalent. In the aftermath of the Acehnese invasion of Johor in 1613, Raja Lela Wangsa of Aceh had sent 2,000 soldiers to garrison Batu Sawar. See also the separate entry for *hikayat*.[465]

Sri (Raja) Mahkota

The title *Serimachi* found in Matelieff's *Journal* may represent a corruption of the Malay title Sri Mahkota, the Crown Prince of Johor. Alternatively but less likely, it could also represent a corruption of Sri Maharaja ('the Great King").[466]

VOC

Vereenigde Oostindische Compagnie (VOC) or the United Netherlands Chartered East India Company, was founded in 1602. The company was formed by merging six regional trading companies and was given a wide range of powers through its charter from the Dutch States General. These included the right to enter into treaties and alliances, wage war, levy troops, build forts, appoint governors, and pronounce justice. After 1619, its administrative center in Asia was in Batavia (formerly known as Jeyakerta or Jacatra) on the northern coast of Java.[467]

---

465 CMJ, 508; L. Andaya, *The Kingdom of Johor 1641-1728: Economic and Political Developments* (Kuala Lumpur: Oxford University Press, 1975), 24.

466 CMJ, 516.

467 CMJ, 523; JCSJ, 109; JDC, 348.

voorcompagnie This Dutch term refers to a precursor company or early Dutch trading partnership that had been active in the East Indies trade between 1595 and 1601. In March 1602, six of these companies merged to form the VOC by transferring existing assets and personnel into the newly formed chartered company and by creating a unified balance sheet. The merger, however, was far from perfect and a relic of these early trading companies were the chambers of the VOC that continued to fund and organize voyages.[468]

---

468 CMJ, 523; R. Parthesius, *Dutch Ships in Tropical Waters. The Development of the Dutch East India Company (VOC) Shipping Network in Asia, 1595-1660* (Amsterdam: Amsterdam University Press, 2010), 32-5; J.C. Boyajian, *Portuguese Trade in Asia under the Habsburgs, 1580-1640* (Baltimore and London: Johns Hopkins University Press, 1993), 326.

List of Place Names

Aru

In the early 16th century, Aru is widely considered in Portuguese sources to be a nation of sea-raiding plunderers. There can be little doubt that it represented, politically and economically, a competitor to both Melaka and later also to Johor. Denys Lombard has reported that Aru had been taken by Aceh in 1564, but the exact status of Aru after this is vague. It would appear that the ruler of Aru refused submission to Aceh or briefly freed himself of it. By the early 17th century it was described as an ally of Johor. Aru was again attacked in 1613 (the same year as Aceh's offensive against Batu Sawar) and it would appear that hereafter a vanquished Aru finally accepted submission to Aceh and was subsequently known as Deli. António Bocarro mentioned the "Isles of Aru" (*ileus Daru*) which appears to refer to the islands located of the eastern coast of Sumatra around Bengkalis.[469] See also the map on p. 19.

Estado da Índia

Literally the "State of India". This term collectively refers to the patchwork of Portuguese colonial dependencies around the Indian Ocean rim and the Western Pacific that were administered from Goa. The Estado da Índia was made up of a string of forts and ports and sometimes larger territories that were subject to different degrees of authority, ranging from

---

469   CMJ, 529; JCSJ, 110; JDC, 351-2; D. Lombard, *Le Sultanat d'Atjéh au temps d'Iskandar Muda 1607-1636* (Paris: École Français d'Extrême-Orient, 1967), 37, 83, 92; A.C. Milner, E. Edwards McKinnon and Tengku Luckman Sinar, "Aru and Kota Cina," *Indonesia*, 26 (1978): 1-42.

outright sovereign possessions to forts and ports under contract with neighbouring Asian or African rulers. The expression is often used interchangeably with "Portuguese India", *Asia Portuguesa*, as well as its colonial administration and bureaucracy.[470]

Jeyakerta   (Also *Jayakarta, Jacatra,* renamed *Batavia* in 1619; present-day *Jakarta*). Before Jeyakerta became the base for the VOC's Asian operations 1619, it was known as Sunda Kelapa and after 1527 as Jeyakerta (Sanskrit for "Complete Victory"). The city rose in the late 16th and early 17th century under Prince Wijayakrama (alias Jayawikarta) who was loyal to Banten and had established his residence near the Ciliwung River estuary. The Prince granted permission to the Dutch in 1610 to establish a wooden warehouse along the right (eastern) bank of the Ciliwung River. Five years later, the East India Company of London (EIC) was granted the same privilege for the left (western) riverbank. The prince's political machinations with the English and the Dutch eventually led to his downfall. The city was taken by the VOC and renamed Batavia in 1619.[471]

Johor Lama   Johor Lama or Old Johor is located on the left bank in the lower reaches of the Johor River. Johor Lama served as the royal residence and capital until it was sacked during a military campaign led by Dom Paulo de Lima Pereira in 1587. Documents of the 17th century report that the city was rebuilt, destroyed again around 1604, and rebuilt a second time. When the Johor court moved to the upstream town of Batu Sawar, Johor Lama continued to be used as

---

470   JCSJ, 102; SMS, 335.
471   CMJ, 447-8; JCSJ, 111-2; JDC, 364.

a port where larger, ocean-going vessels would anchor and transfer their cargo to smaller vessels (for example *perahus* or *sampans*). From here, the goods were brought to the upstream towns such as the royal administrative center Batu Sawar and the settlement of Kota Seberang nearby on the opposite bank of the Johor River.[472]

Karimun (Also: *Carimon* and other spellings.) There are technically two Karimuns, Karimun Besar (Great Carimon) and the far smaller and uninhabited Karimun Kecil (Carimon Minor). The Karimuns are located between the great island of Sumatra and the Malay Peninsula. The islands are strategically located, as several major shipping routes converge around them, including significantly the Singapore, Melaka, Durian and Kundur Straits (the latter being known as the Strait of Sabam from Portuguese source materials).[473]

Maluku (Also: *Maluco*; Moluccas, Spice Islands). Subgroup of the Indonesian Archipelago located between the two great islands of Sulawesi (Celebes) and Papua (New Guinea) and comprising, among others, the clove and nutmeg producing islands of Ambon, Aru, Banda, Buru, Halmahera, Seram, Ternate and Tidore. The region is ethnically and culturally diverse, featuring Malay, Papuan and other influences. The islands were contested by the Portuguese and the Spanish, who sought to claim and extend their influence over the islands. In the early 17th century, the contest for the Malukus involved the Dutch, who eventually came to dominate the entire archipelago and monop-

---

472   CMJ, 549; JDC, 365; SMS, 343.
473   CMJ, 550-1; JCSJ, 112; JDC, 376; SMS, 343.

olised the spice trade in nutmeg, mace (a by-product of nutmeg) and cloves.[474]

Mozambique   Historically, the toponym Mozambique refers to an island, a region of southeastern Africa, a country, as well as a channel or strait located between the southeast African mainland and the great island of Madagascar. In the early modern period, the toponym referred first and foremost to an island by that name which was occupied by the Portuguese and home to the fort *São Sebastião* (Saint Sebastian). The neighbouring Portuguese settlement on the island was also known as Stone Town, because just a few hundred metres away there was another settlement of wood and perishable materials inhabited by African slaves and Swahili mariners. The name was also applied to the nearby region of southeastern Africa, hence the country of Mozambique. The Mozambique Channel between the southeastern coast of Africa and Madagascar derives its name from the adjacent country on the African mainland.[475] See the illustration on p. 137.

New Strait of   (Portuguese: *Estreito Novo*). The New Strait of
Singapore   Singapore was a maritime route that, according to the testimony of João de Barros, opened up after the 1580s when Johor had blockaded the Old Strait (see the separate entry below) with logs, debris and sunken vessels. This route, also known from João de Barros in Portuguese as the *Estreito de Santa Bárbara* (Strait of Santa Bárbara), brought vessels during the age of sail along the southwestern coast of present-day Sentosa and then either through the Buran

---

474   CMJ, 557; JCSJ, 113; JDC, 368; SMS, 343.
475   CMJ, 562-3; JDC, 370.

Channel or around the southern islands and on to the region of the Johor River estuary.[476]

Old Strait of Singapore (Portuguese: *Estreito Velho*). The western entrance to the Old Strait of Singapore begins at the site of present-day Fort Siloso (on the Sentosa side) and the *Varella* (also Longyamen, Sail Rock, Batu Belayer, Batu Blair, Lot's Wife) in today's Labrador Park. It continued through the narrow maritime passage between present-day Sentosa and the Keppel Harbor area and ended after Pulau Brani.[477]

Patani Port and polity located on the Isthmus of Kra at the Gulf of Siam in present-day Thailand. Descriptions of the polity dating from the late 16th and early 17th century claim that most of the eastern coast of the Malay Peninsula fell under the control of Patani, being chiefly around the present-day Malaysian States of Kelantan and Terengganu. Many Chinese came to trade in Patani and brought a range of trading goods such as silks, copperware, and porcelain. The town manufactured, among other things, finished clothing which were exported to and very much prized in Banda and the Maluku islands.[478]

Pulau Butom (Sometimes also Pulobotum and other spellings). A small archipelago (today's Mu Ko A Dang-Ra Wi) located to the northwest of Langkawi in present-day Tarutao National Park, Satun Province, Thailand. The name *Butom* appears to represent a corruption of the name [*Koh*] *Butang* which today is the name of the third largest island in the group and is sep-

---

476   CMJ, 578; JCSJ, 114-5; JDC, 360-1; SMS, 31-2
477   CMJ, 578; JCSJ, 115; JDC, 361; SMS, 26-35.
478   CMJ, 567-8; JCSJ, 115; JDC, 373.

arated by a channel located to the southwest of Koh Ra Wi. The islands were known as a place to fetch fresh water and collect firewood. The two principal islands A Dang and Ra Wi form together a protected, bay-like opening that is open toward the south. The two islands are separated by a channel that reportedly features strong currents. The *Journal* provides a fairly detailed description of the topographic features noting also: "Pulau Butom comprises many islands, most importantly two big ones [present-day Ko Ra Wi and Ko A Dang] with a passage in-between that stretches north and south. The east island of that passage [Ko A Dang] has a sandy bay [located on the northeast side of the island] with a big recess, which moreover has a point [present-day Laem Tan Yong Baku] jutting out with rocks and cliffs, so that ships lying in the bay are protected from the north and northeast wind."[479]

Pulau Condor This name refers to a small archipelago known in Vietnamese as Côn Đảo. The toponym may represent a corruption of the Malay name Pulau Kundur (and should not to be confused with the present-day Pulau Kundur in the Riau Archipelago). It is located off the southern coast of Vietnam. In early modern times, the main island Pulau Condor (Côn Sơn) was an important station to bring on water and provisions before ships set in a southwestern direction across the Gulf of Siam toward the island of Tioman or Pulau Aor. Due to its significance as a station along the long-distance shipping routes between the Malay Peninsula and China, Pulau Condor was the object of colonial acquisition. In the early 17th century, the Dutch at

---

479   CJM, 571-2; JDC, 377.

one stage toyed with the idea of establishing their rendezvous here, Pulau Condor briefly hosted failed attempts by the British and French to acquire and garrison the island. Farrington and Pombejra noted that Pulau Condor had been "occupied by the English in 1703 in an attempt to create an independent base for the China trade, but the settlers were massacred by the Bugis mercenaries they [i.e. the English] had employed as their garrison."[480]

Shabandaria   (Also: *Sabandaria*, *Xabandaria* and other spellings). This is the name given by Jacques de Coutre to the principal settlement on what he calls the *Isla de la Sabandaría Vieja* (Island of the Old Shahbandar's Compound; present-day Singapore Island). According to his information, the settlement was located near the eastern entrance of the *Estrecho Viejo* (Old Strait of Singapore). He claimed that its inhabitants paid allegiance to the king of Johor. He also underscored that *Sabandaría*'s harbor was one of the best in all of the East Indies. The exact location of the settlement is unclear but it would have most likely been either at the site of Raffles' Landing Place or possibly also nearby around the Kallang River estuary.[481]

South   The Portuguese and the Spanish generically employed this term to refer to what today would be Southeast Asia, especially the insular portions of Indonesia and the Philippines. From the vantage point of the Portuguese administration in Goa, this region was located in the "South". Contemporary historians have variously translated this term into English either as "the South" (corresponding literally

---

480   CMJ, 572; EFS, II, 1408; SMS, 344.
481   JCSJ, 116; JDC, 378.

to the Portuguese *Sul* or the Spanish *Sur*), "the East Indies", or occasionally also as Southeast Asia.[482]

---

482   CMJ, 579; JCSJ, 116; JDC, 381.

Bibliography

Amsterdam, Rijksmuseum

M-SK-A-1469-00 Portrait of Pieter Willemsz. Verhoeff (artist unknown).

RP-B-OP-47.821 Etching of Palembang, D. de Jong. (artist unknown).

RP-P-OB-80.246 Etching of Banten's bazaar, 1596 (artist unknown).

RP-T-00-1284 Portrait of Steven van der Hagen, P.M.A. Schouman.

SK-A-255-00 Portrait of Prince Maurice, M.J. van Mierevelt.

SK-A-3108 East Indiamen, H.C. Vroom.

SK-A-3741 Portrait of Laurens Reael, C. van der Voort.

SK-A-4070 East Indian market stall, A. Eckhout.

SK-A-4491-00 Portrait of Cornelis Matelieff de Jonge by P. van der Werff, c.1699.

SK-A-4528-00 Copy portrait of Jan Pietersz. Coen (artist unknown).

The Hague, Nationaal Archief van Nederland

Collectie Hugo de Groot Supplement, access code 1.10.35.02, no. 40.

Collectie Johan van Oldenbarnevelt, access code 3.01.14, no. 3104.

Vereenigde Oostindische Compagnie, 1602-1795, ms. cod. 100, access code 1.04.02, no. 100.

Lisbon, Arquivo Nacional da Torre do Tombo (ANTT)
Colecção São Vicente, livro XXVI, fol. 130 recto-130 verso.

Rotterdam, Gemeentearchief
Ms. cod. 33.01, no. 3366, Stukken betreffende de handel en scheepvaart op Indië, 1603-13."
Ms. cod. 33.01, no. 3367, "Derde discours omtrent de stand van zaken in Oost-Indië door Cornelis Matelieff de Jonge overgeleverd aan den advocaat Mr. Johan van Oldenbarnevelt op 23 Mei 1609."

An historicall and true discourse, of a voyage made by the Admirall Cornelis Matelife the yonger, into the East Indies, who departed out of Holland, in May 1605: With the besieging of Malacca, and the battaile by him fought at sea against the Portugales in the Indies, with other discourses. Translated out of the Dutch, according to the coppie printed at Rotterdam, 1608 (Imprinted at London for William Barret, and are to be sold at his shop in Paules Church-yard, at the signe of the greene Dragon, 1608)

Catalogue des Manuscrits Autographes de Hugo Grotius. Vente à La Haye, 15 Novembre 1864, sous la direction et au domicile de Martinus Nijhoff. The Hague: Martinus Nijhoff, 1864.

Journael Ende Historische Verhael/ van de treffelijcke Reyse/ gedaen naer Oost-Indien, ende China, met elf Schepen, Door den Manhaften Admirael Cornelis Matelieff de Jonge. Uyt-ghevaren in den Jare 1605. En wat haer in de volgende Jaren 1606, 1607, ende 1608 weder-varen is. Een seer Vreemde en Wonderlijcke Reyse. t' Amstelredam: Door Joost Hartgers, Boeck-verkooper in de Gasthuys-Steegh, bezijden het Stadt-huys, in de Boeck-winckel, 1648.

Relação das Plantas & Descripções de todas as Fortalezas, Cidades & Povoações que os Portuguezes tem no Estado da India Oriental. Lisbon: Biblioteca Nacional, 1936.

VOC Glossarium. Verklaringen van Termen, verzamelt uit de Rijksgeschiedkundige Publicatiën die betrekking hebben op de Verenigde Oost-Indische Compagnie. The Hague: Instituut voor Nederlandse Geschiedenis, 2000.

Akveld, L., ed. *Machtstrijd om Malakka.* Zutphen: Walburg Pers, 2013.

Albuquerque, B. de, *Comentarios de Afonso d'Albuqerque.* Edited by J. Veríssimo Serrão, and int., text of the 2nd edition of 1576, 2 vols. Lisbon: Imprensa Nacional-Casa de Moeda, 1973.

―――. *Commentaries of the Great Afonso Dalboquerque, Second Viceroy of India.* Edited and translated by W. de Gray Birch, 4 vols. London: Hakluyt Society, 1880.

Alexandrowicz, C.H., ed. *Grotian Society Papers 1968. Studies in the History of the Law of Nations.* The Hague: Martinus Nijhoff, 1970.

Ali al-Haji ibn Ahmad. *The Precious Gift/ Tuhfat al-Nafis.* Edited and translated by V.M. Hooker and Barbara Watson Andaya. Kuala Lumpur and New York: Oxford University Press, 1982.

Andaya, L.Y. *Leaves of the Same Tree: Trade and Ethnicity in the Straits of Melaka.* Honolulu: Hawai'i University Press, 2008.

―――. *The Kingdom of Johor 1641-1728: Economic and Political Developments.* Kuala Lumpur: Oxford University Press, 1975.

Barros, J. de, and D. do Couto. *Da Ásia. Dos feitos que os Portuguezes fizeram no conquista, e descubrimento das terras e mares do Oriente,* 26 vols. Lisbon: Na Regia Officina Typographia, 1778.

Benda, H.J. "The Structure of Southeast Asian History: Some Preliminary Observations." *Journal of Southeast Asian History,* 3, 1 (1962): 106-38.

Bijlsma, R. "De discoursen van Cornelis Matelieff de Jonge over den Staat van Oost-Indië." *Nederlandsch Archievenblad*, 35 (1927-8): 49-53.

Bok, M.J. "European Artists in the Service of the Dutch East India Company." In *Mediating Netherlandish Art and Material Culture in Asia*, edited by T. DaCosta Kaufmann and M. North, 177-204. Amsterdam: Amsterdam University Press, 2014.

Booy, A. de, ed. *De derde reis van de V.O.C. naar Oost-Indië onder het beleid van Admiraal Paulus van Caerden, uitgezeild in 1606*, 2 vols. The Hague: Martinus Nijhoff, 1970.

Borschberg, Peter. *Hugo Grotius, the Portuguese and Free Trade in the East Indies*. Singapore and Leiden: NUS Press and KITLV Press, 2011.

―――. *The Singapore and Melaka Straits: Violence, Security and Diplomacy in the 17th Century*. Singapore and Leiden: NUS Press and KITLV Press, 2010.

―――, ed. *The Memoirs and Memorials of Jacques de Coutre. Security, Trade and Society in 17th Century Southeast Asia*. Singapore: NUS Press, 2014.

―――, ed. *Jacques de Coutre's Singapore and Johor (c.1594-1625)*. Singapore: NUS Press, 2015.

―――, ed. *Journal, Memorials and Letters of Cornelis Matelieff de Jonge: Security, Diplomacy and Commerce in 17th-Century Southeast Asia*. Singapore: NUS Press, 2015.

―――. "The Euro-Asian Trade in Bezoar Stones (approx. 1500-1700)." In *Artistic and Cultural Exchanges between Europe and Asia, 1400-1900: Rethinking Markets, Workshops and Collections*, edited by T. DaCosta Kaufmann and M. North, 29-43. Aldershot: Ashgate, 2010.

―――. "The Euro-Asian Trade and Medicinal Usage of Radix Chinae." In *European Travellers and the Asian Natural World, Part 1*, edited by Rui Manuel Loureiro. Revista de Cultura, International Edition, 20 (2006): 102-115.

―――. "From Self-Defense to an Instrument of War: Dutch Privateering Around the Malay Peninsula in the Early

Seventeenth Century." *Journal of Early Modern History*, 17 (2013): 35-52.

———. "Left 'Holding the Bag': The Johor-VOC Alliance and the Twelve Years Truce (1606-1609)." In *The Twelve Years Truce (1609). Peace, Truce, War and Law in the Low Countries at the Turn of the 17th Century*, edited by Randall Lesaffer, 89-120. Leiden: Brill-Nijhoff, 2014.

———, ed. *Iberians in the Singapore-Melaka Area and Adjacent Regions.* Wiesbaden and Lisbon: Harrassowitz and Fundação Oriente, 2009.

———. "Portuguese, Spanish and Dutch plans to construct a Fort in the Straits of Singapore ca 1584-1625." *Archipel*, 63 (2003): 55-88.

———. "The Euro-Asian Trade and Medicinal Usage of Radix Chinae." *Revista de Cultura*, International Edition, 20 (2006): 102-15.

———. "The Seizure of the Sta. Catarina Revisited: The Portuguese Empire in Asia, VOC Politics and the Origins of the Dutch-Johor Alliance (c. 1602-1616)." *JSEAS*, 33.1 (2002): 31-62.

———. "The Seizure of the Santa Catarina off Singapore: Dutch Freebooting, the Portuguese Empire and Intra-Asian Trade at the Dawn of the Seventeenth Century." *Revista de Cultura*, International Edition, 11 (2004): 11-25.

———. "The Straits of Singapore: Continuity, Change and Confusion." In *Sketching the Straits: A Compilation of the Lecture Series on the Charles Dyce Collection*, edited by I. Lim, 33-47. Singapore: NUS Museums, 2004.

———. "The Trade, Forgery and Medicinal Use of Porcupine Bezoars in the Early Modern Period (c. 1500-1750)." *Revista Oriente*, 14 (2006): 60-78.

Boyajian, J.C. *Portuguese Trade in Asia under the Habsburgs, 1580-1640.* Baltimore and London: Johns Hopkins University Press, 1993.

Bulbeck, D., A. Reid, Lay Cheng Tan and Wu Yiqi, ed. *Southeast Asian Exports since the 14th Century: Cloves, Pepper, Coffee and Sugar.* Singapore: ISEAS, 1998.

Caminha, A.L. ed. *Ordenações da Índia do Senhor Rei D. Manoel, etc.* Lisbon: Na Impressão Regia, 1807.

Chauvel, R. "Ambon's Other Half: Some Preliminary Observations on Ambonese Society and History." *Review of Indonesian and Malaysian Affairs*, 14.1 (1980): 40-80.

Cheah B.K. and P. Borschberg. "Raja Bongsu and Sejarah Melayu (The Malay Annals): An 'ill-starred prince' of Johor with a tragic fate (b.1571- d.1623)." *JMBRAS*, 2016, forthcoming.

Chijs, J.A. van der, ed. *Nederlandsch-Indisch Plakaatboek, 1602-1811*, 17 vols. Batavia: Landsdrukkerij, and The Hague: Martinus Nijhoff, 1885-1900.

Colenbrander, H.T., and W.Ph. Coolhaas, ed. *Jan Pieterszoon Coen: Bescheiden Omtrent Zijn Bedrijf in Indië*, 9 vols. The Hague: Martinus Nijhoff, 1919-53.

Commelin, I. *Begin ende Voortgang vande Vereenigde Neerlandsche Geoctroyeerde Oost-Indische Compagnie*, 4 vols., facsimile of the original edition of 1646 in 2 vols. Amsterdam: Facsimile Uitgaven Nederland, 1969.

Cortesão, A., and Avelino Teixeira da Mota. *Portugaliae Monumenta Cartographica*, 9 vols. Lisbon: Imprensa Nacional-Casa da Moeda, 1987.

Crawfurd, J. *History of the Indian Archipelago*, facsimile edition printed by Archibald Constable & Co., Edinburgh, 1820, 3 vols. London: Frank Cass, 1967.

Cruysse, D. van der. *Siam and the West, 1500-1700.* Chiang Mai: Silkworm Books, 2002.

DaCosta Kaufmann, T., and M. North, ed. *Mediating Netherlandish Art and Material Culture in Asia.* Amsterdam: Amsterdam University Press, 2014.

Dalgado, S.R. *Glosário Luso-Asiático*, 2 vols. Coimbra: Imprensa da Universidade, 1919-21.

Dam, P. van. *Beschryvinge van de Oostindische Compagnie.* Edited by F.W. Stapel, 8. vols. The Hague: Martinus Nijhoff, 1931-43.

Day, T. *Fluid Iron. State Formation in Southeast Asia.* Honolulu: Hawai'i University Press, 2002.

Drakard, J. *A Kingdom of Words. Language and Power in Sumatra.* Oxford: Oxford University Press, 1999.

Dunlop, H., ed. *Bronnen tot de Geschiedenis der Oostindische Compagnie in Perzië, eerste deel, 1611-1638.* The Hague: Martinus Nijhoff, 1930.

Duyvendak, J.J.L. "The First Siamese Embassy to Holland." *T'oung Pao,* 32 (1936): 285-92.

Erédia, M. Godinho de. *Informação da Aurea Quersoneso, ou Península, e das Ilhas Auríferas, Carbúculas e Aromáticas.* Edited by R.M. Loureiro. Macau: Centro Científico e Cultural de Macau, 2008.

———. *Description of Malaca, Meridional India and Cathay. Translated from the Portuguese with Notes.* Translated and edited by J.V.G. Mills. Kuala Lumpur: MBRAS, 1997.

———. *Malaca, l'Inde Méridionale e le Cathay: Manuscrit original autographe de Godinho de Eredia appartenant à la Bibliothèque Royale de Bruxelles.* Translated by M. Léon Janssen. Bruxelles: Librairie Européenne C. Muquardt, 1882.

———. "Informação da Aurea Chersoneso." In *Ordenações da Índia do Senhor Rei D. Manoel, etc.* Edited by A.L. Caminha, 65-151. Lisbon: Na Impressão Regia, 1807.

Farrington, A., and Dhiravat na Pombejra, ed. *The English Factory in Siam, 1612-1685,* 2 vols. London: The British Library, 2007.

Fitch, R. *Early Travels in India, 1583-1619.* Edited by W. Foster. London: Humphrey Milsford and Oxford University Press, 1921.

Foster, W., ed. *The Voyage of Thomas Best to the East Indies 1612-1614.* London: Hakluyt Society, 1934.

227

Frederiks, J.G. "Cornelis Cornelisz Matelieff de Jonge en zijn geslagt." *Rotterdamsche Historiebladen*, J.H. Scheffer and Fr. D.O. Obreen, ed., 3 afd., 1.1 (1871): 204-357.

Gaastra, F.S. *The Dutch East India Company. Expansion and Decline*. Zutphen, Walburg Pers, 2003.

Gibson-Hill, C.A. "The Alleged Death of Sultan 'Ala'udin of Johor at Acheh in 1613." *JMBRAS* 29, 1 (1956): 125-45.

Grotius, H. *De Jure Belli ac Pacis*. Translated by F.W. Kelsey and edited by J.B. Scott, reprint of the original edition of 1925. New York: Oceana Publications, 1964.

———. *Jure Praedae Commentarius: Commentary on the Law of Prize and Booty*. Edited by M.J. van Ittersum (Indianapolis: Liberty Fund, 2006).

———. *De Jure Praedae Commentarius. Commentary on the Law of Prize and Booty. A Translation of the Original Manuscript of 1604*. Translated by G.L. Williams and W.H. Zeydel. Oxford: Clarendon Press, 1950.

———. *The Free Sea*. Translated by Richard Hakluyt, edited and introduced by D. Armitage. Indianapolis: Liberty Fund, 2004.

Gullick, J.M. *Indigenous Political Systems of Western Malaya*. London: The Athlone Press, 1958.

Hägerdal, H. *Responding to the West: Essays on Colonial Domination and Asian Agency*. Amsterdam: Amsterdam University Press, 2009.

Hall, K.R. "Upstream and Downstream Unification in Southeast Asia's First Islamic Polity: The Changing Sense of Community in the Fifteenth Century 'Hikayat Raja-Raja Pasai' Court Chronicle." *Journal of the Economic and Social History of the Orient*, 44.2 (2001): 198-229.

Heryanto, A. "Can there be Southeast Asians in Southeast Asian Studies?" In *Knowing Southeast Asian Subjects*, edited by L.J. Sears, 75-108. Seattle and Singapore: University of Washington Press and NUS Press, 2007.

Hoesein Djajadiningrat. *Critische beschouwing van de Sadjarah Bantĕn: Bijdrage ter kenschetsing van de Javaansche geschiedschrijving.* Haarlem: Joh. Enschedé en Zonen, 1913.

Jonge, J.K.J. de. *Opkomst van het Nederlandsch gezag in Oost-Indië: Verzameling van onuitgegeven stukken uit het oud-coloniaal archief,* 16 vols. The Hague: Martinus Nijhoff, 1866-1925.

Korte, J.P. de. *The Annual Accounting in the VOC, the English Companion to De Korte, De jaarlijkse financiële verantwoording in de VOC.* Translated by L.F. van Lookeren Campagne-de Korte. Amsterdam: NEHA, 2000.

Legge, J. "The Writing of Southeast Asian History." In *The Cambridge History of Southeast Asia,* vol. 1, edited by N. Tarling, 1-50. Cambridge: Cambridge University Press, 1992.

Leupe, P.G. "The Siege and Capture of Malacca from the Portuguese in 1640-1641. Extracts from the Archives of the Dutch East India Company." Translated by Mac Hacobian. *JMBRAS,* 14.1 (1936): 1-178.

Lim, I., ed. *Sketching the Straits. A Compilation of the Lecture Series on the Charles Dyce Collection.* Singapore: NUS Museums, 2004.

Linschoten, J.H. van. Itinerario. *Voyage ofte Schipvaert van Jan Huygen van Linschoten naer Oost ofte Portugaels Indien, 1579-1592, and Reys-geschrift vande navigatiën der Portugaloysers.* Edited by H. Kern and J.C.M. Warnsinck, 2nd ed., 8 vols. The Hague: Martinus Nijhoff, 1939.

Lombard, D. *Le Sultanat d'Atjéh au temps d'Iskandar Muda 1607-1636.* Paris: École Français d'Extrême-Orient, 1967.

Meilink-Roelofsz, M.A.P. *Asian Trade and European Influence in the Indonesian Archipelago between 1500 and about 1630.* The Hague: Martinus Nijhoff, 1962.

Miksic, J.N., ed. *Archaeological Research on the 'Forbidden Hill' of Singapore: Excavations at Fort Canning.* Singapore: National Museum, 1984.

Milner, A.C. *The Malays.* Oxford: Wiley-Blackwell, 2008.

————. *The Invention of Politics in Colonial Malaya: Contesting Nationalism and the Expansion of Public Space*. Cambridge: Cambridge University Press, 1995.

————. Kerajaan. *Malay Political Culture on the Eve of Colonial Rule*. Tucson: The University of Arizona Press, 1982.

————. "Colonial Records History: British Malaya." *Modern Asian Studies*, 21, 4 (1987): 773-92.

Milner, A.C., E. Edwards McKinnon and Tengku Luckman Sinar. "Aru and Kota Cina." *Indonesia*, 26 (1978): 1-42.

Moreland, W.H., ed. *Pieter Floris: His Voyage to the East Indies in the Globe, 1611-1615*. London: Hakluyt Society, 1934.

Muhammad Yusof Hashim. *The Malay Sultanate of Malacca*. Translated by D.J. Muzaffar Tate. Kuala Lumpur: Dewan Bahasa dan Pustaka, 1992.

Naber, S.P. l'Honoré, ed. *Reisebeschreibungen von Deutschen Beamten und Kriegsleuten im Dienst der Niederländisch West- und Ost-Indischen Kompanien, 1602-1797*, 13 vols. The Hague: Martinus Nijhoff, 1930-33.

Nellen, H.J.M. *Hugo Grotius, A Lifelong Struggle for Peace in Church and State, 1583-1645*. Leiden: Brill, 2014.

Nellen, H.J.M. ed., *Briefwisseling van Hugo Grotius, zeventiende deel, Supplement 1583-1645*, with the addenda compiled by C.M. Ridderikhoff. The Hague: Instituut voor Nederlandse Geschiedenis, 2001.

Noordhoff, L.J. *Beschrijving van het zich in Nederland bevindende en nog onbeschreven gedeelte der papieren afkomstig van Huig de Groot welke in 1864 te 's-Gravenhage zijn geveild*. Groningen-Djakarta: Noordhoff, 1953.

North, M., ed. *Artistic and Cultural Exchanges between Europe and Asia, 1400-1900: Rethinking Markets, Workshops and Collections*. Aldershot: Ashgate, 2010.

Opstall, M.E. van. *De reis van de vloot van Pieter Willemsz Verhoeff naar Azië, 1607–1612*, 2 vols. The Hague: Martinus Nijhoff, 1972.

Orta, G. de. *Colloquies on the Simple and Drugs of India.* Translated by C. Mackham. Delhi: Sri Satguru Publications, 1987.

Parthesius, R. *Dutch Ships in Tropical Waters. The Development of the Dutch East India Company (VOC) Shipping Network in Asia, 1595-1660.* Amsterdam: Amsterdam University Press, 2010.

Pelliot, P. "Les Relations du Siam et de la Hollande en 1608." *T'oung Pao*, 32 (1936): 223-9.

Pinto, P.J. de Sousa. *The Portuguese and the Straits of Melaka, 1575-1619. Power, Trade and Diplomacy.* Singapore: NUS Press, 2012.

–––. "Captains, Sultans and liaisons dangereuses: Melaka and Johor in the Late Sixteenth Century." In *Iberians in the Singapore-Melaka Area and Adjacent Regions.* Edited by Peter Borschberg, 131-46. Wiesbaden and Lisbon: Harrassowitz and Fundação Oriente, 2009.

Pires, T. *The Suma Oriental of Tome Pires. An Account of the East from the Red Sea to Japan. Written in Malacca and India in 1512-1515*, 2 vols. Edited by Armando Cortesão. London: Hakluyt Society, 1944.

Rietbergen, P.J.A.N. van. *De Eerste Landvoogd Pieter Both (1568-1615): Gouverneur-Generaal van Nederlandsch-Indië*, 2 vols. Zutphen: Walberg Pers, 1987.

Rouffaer, P.G. "Was Malaka Emporium vóór 1400 A.D. genaamd Malajoer? En waar lag Woerawari, Ma-Hasin, Langka, Batoesawar?" *Bijdragen en Mededelingen van het Koninklijk Instituut voor Taal-, Land- und Volkenkunde*, 77 (1921): 1-174 and 359-604.

Roux, P. le, B. Sellato and J. Ivanoff, ed. *Poids e mesures en Asie du Sud-Est – Weights and Measures in Southeast Asia*, 2 vols. Paris: École française de l'Extrême-Orient and Institut de Recherche sur le Sud-Est Asiatique, 2004-8.

Rubin, A.P. "The Use of Piracy in Malayan Waters." In *Grotian*

Society Papers 1968. Studies in the History of the Law of Nations. Edited by C.H. Alexandrowicz, 111-35. The Hague: Martinus Nijhoff, 1970.

Satow, E.M., ed. *The Voyage of Captain John Saris to Japan, 1613.* London: Hakluyt Society, 1900.

Sears, L.J., ed. *Knowing Southeast Asian Subjects.* Seattle and Singapore: University of Washington Press and NUS Press, 2007.

Sircar, D.C. *Studies in the Geography of Ancient and Medieval India.* Delhi: Shanti Lal Jain, 1971.

Smail, J.R.W. "On the Possibility of an Autonomous History of Modern Southeast Asia." *Journal of Southeast Asian History,* 2 (1961): 72-102.

Sopher, D.E. *The Sea Nomads, a Study Based on Literature of the Maritime Boat People of Southeast Asia.* Singapore: Lim Bian Han, 1965.

Tarling, N., ed. *The Cambridge History of Southeast Asia,* 2 vols. Cambridge: Cambridge University Press, 1992.

Tex, J. den. *Oldenbarnevelt,* 2 vols. Cambridge: Cambridge University Press, 1974.

Tiele, P.A. "De Europeërs in den Maleischen Archipel." Part VII, *Bijdragen en Mededelingen van het Koninklijk Instituut voor Taal-, Land- und Volkenkunde,* 32 (1884): 49-118.

————. *Mémoire bibliographique sur les journaux des navigateurs néerlandais réimprimés dans les collections de De Bry et de Hulsius, et dans les collections hollandaises du XVIIe siècle, et sur les anciennes éditions hollandaises des journaux de navigateurs étrangers; la plupart en la possession de Frederik Muller a Amsterdam.* Amsterdam: Frederik Muller, 1867.

Wickeren, A. van. *Geschiedenis van Portugal en van Portugezen overzee,* part XVI. Heerhugowaart: no publisher, 2007.

Wolters, O.W. *Early Indonesian Commerce: A Study of the Origins of Srivijaya.* Ithaca: Cornell University Press, 1967.

Yule, H., and A.C. Burnell. *Hobson-Jobson: A Glossary of Colloquial Anglo-Indian Words and Phrases*, reprint. Sittingbourne: Linguasia, 1994.

Index

Laksamana, 23-5, 76, 78, 81, 84,
138, 200
Land, 29-31, 33, 37, 45, 49,
58, 60, 64, 75, 78, 90, 96-7,
99-100, 108-11, 113-5, 118,
125, 128, 132, 134, 136, 139,
143, 155, 157-8, 161-2, 168,
174, 179,184, 187, 191, 193-4,
206, 208
Land's Advocate of Holland,15,
117
Landak, 73, 152
Lantau Island, 8
Lawai, 73
Legge, J., 26
Leiden University Library, 3, 48
Leupe, P.G., 20. 10
Lim, I., 39
Lingga, 110, 119
Linschoten, J.H. van, 137, 202-3
Lobato, M., 22
Lombard, D., 213
Lontor, 123
Loureiro, R.M., 22
Luhu, 126

Macao, 138, 166, 173, 186
Mace, 5, 69, 82, 123, 125, 158,
205-6, 209, 216
Makian, 203
Malabar Coast, 129, 132, 159
Malay Peninsula, 8-9, 19, 29, 40,
44, 49, 57, 65, 75, 87, 93, 116,
147, 159
Malay rulers, 26, 28
Malayo (Ternate), 5
Malays, 29, 61, 79, 94, 104, 107,
114, 136
Malaysia, 62, 89, 217
Maluku, 5, 45, 54, 57, 82, 97, 119,
123, 126-7, 135-6, 138, 141-2,
147-8, 175, 192, 203, 215-7
Mandarin, 67, 206
Manila, 122, 126-7, 142-3
Martaban, 209

Masulipatam, 128
Maurice of Nassau, 12, 91, 13,
170, 189-92, 195
McKinnon, E., 213
Megat Mansur, 189, 192
Meilink-Roelofsz, M.A.P., 22
Meissen, 197
Melaka sultanate, 20-1, 23-4, 199
Mempawah, 73
Mendonça, A. Furtado de, 113,
118, 137
Meneses, A. de, 118
Meneses, D. de, 118
Middelburg, 204-5
Miervelt, M.J. van, 190-1
Milner, A., 26, 75, 78, 213
Min Razagri, 132
Mindanao, 126-7
Moelre, J. de, 159
Moghul, 124
Mohammad Yusof Hashim, 20,
22-3, 199-200
Mon, 116
Moreland, W.H., 129, 207
Moti, 203
Mozambique, 8, 135, 137, 159,
163, 216
Mrauk-U (Myanmar), 132
Mu Ko A Dang-Ra Wi, 217
Muar, 89, 118
Muller, F., 14
Muslim, 125, 153, 155, 160, 200
Myanmar (Burma), 132, 161

Naber, S.P.H. de, 197
Nagapattinam, 128-31
Nan'ao Dao (China), 8
National Archives of the
Netherlands, 5, 13-5, 54-5, 69,
111, 129, 132, 154
Nawab of Bengal, 124
Negeri, 18, 20, 77-8, 136, 191
Nellen, H.J.M., 11, 44, 154
Netscher, E., 81, 177, 182
New Strait of Singapore (Strait